VIDEO DEMOCRACY

VIDEO DEMOCRACY

The
Vote – from – Home
Revolution

RICHARD S. HOLLANDER

Lomond Publications, Inc.

ISBN: 0-912338-51-2
         0-912338-52-0 (Microfiche)

Library of Congress Catalog No. 85-081818

Set in Compugraphic Paladium type by Brown Graphics, Damascus, Md.

Book design by Laura L. Nagy.

To my parents

CONTENTS

ACKNOWLEDGMENTS

IT IS CUSTOMARY for an author to acknowledge those who helped transform random thoughts into a completed book. In this case, it is not just customary, but essential. I am especially indebted to Laura Nagy, a truly gifted editor. I am grateful for the assistance of Sister Ian Stewart, Director of the Loyola-Notre Dame Library in Baltimore, for giving me a place where I could put my thoughts on paper. She and her professional staff showed me every kindness. I would further like to express my gratitude to the management of WBAL-TV in Baltimore for giving me time for this project. My colleagues in the news department deserve special thanks for picking up the slack when I was involved in the research and writing of the manuscript. Finally, I wish to acknowledge the contribution of my most perceptive critic, my wife, Ellen. Her support, patience, and good humor, along with that of our children, Hillary, Craig, and Brett, made everything possible.

R. H.
Baltimore, Maryland
June 1985

INTRODUCTION

THE TIME IS the day after tomorrow.

The hour is not so close that we can see it clearly. It is not so far that it is fantasy.

The video revolution has arrived in America, a revolution that has its roots in today's technology. It is to be seen in the geo-stationary communications satellites soaring twenty-three thousand miles above the earth; in miniscule silicon chips storing untold libraries of information; in hair-thin drawn glass strands called optical fibers, capable of carrying the knowledge of the world in pulses of light.

To observers in the 1980s, the video revolution is primarily one of communications. The new technology cements the relationship of the two most important technological achievements of the mid-twentieth-century world—television and the computer. From today forward the two technologies of video and information management are to be married.

Looking back a generation from now, it will be obvious that the marriage of the TV and the computer has left its imprint on every American household. In that not-so-far-off time, scarcely a family can be found who doesn't belong to the video revolution. Each TV home is connected by the cable umbilical to an earth station—a large metallic dish capable of bringing down to earth the multitude of broadcast transmissions bouncing off communications satellites. And within each home, attached to every television, is a computer.

No one *watches* TV anymore. Everyone *participates* in television. Television has quite literally become a member of the family. Every facet of life changed when the two-way cable entered the American home back in the 1980s and early 1990s. It changed the way food was

1

cooked; children were raised; bills were paid; livelihoods were earned; medicine was practiced, and it even left its mark on people's sex lives. The TV/computer was there from the time people woke up until the time they went to sleep. And while they slept, the box in the living room watched the house, monitoring temperature and humidity, sniffing the air for fire, and scanning the windows for burglars.

The TV/computer became the perfect slave and the perfect master.

It would be folly to believe that such a radical transformation in lifestyle can occur without its effects spilling into the world of politics.

There is nothing profound about that. The story has been written before. It was carved on the walls of neolithic caves; it was inscribed on papyrus along the banks of the Nile; it was written into long-decayed medieval manuscripts; it went up in smoke from Indian campfires on the Great Plains; it found its way into pamphlets, books, and newspapers and ultimately rode the airwaves into radios and televisions. The lesson is clear: Every technological advance that changes communications must, by definition, change politics.

If popular government is a worthy end, no democratic society should stay rooted in the sands of history. As the technology cannot—and will not—be denied, neither can the new political reality. Democratic societies must accept change and then mold their institutions appropriately. The argument here is that the new technology can invigorate a political system which sometimes borders on the stale and generally fails to achieve the noble end of public participation. The technology is not to be feared, but neither is it to be ignored.

Since the founding of the Republic, the United States has been an *indirect* democracy. The ancient Athenian model of direct citizen participation and the dreams of the democrats of the Enlightenment were necessarily scrapped for a less cumbersome system. The indirect democratic system adopted under the Constitution was not only practical, but also meshed magnificently with the philosophic orientation of the Founders. For reasons to be discussed later, the Founders were far more concerned about the threat from the mob than the preservation of true democracy.

The video revolution promises to turn the world of the Founders on its head. Indirect democracy—or representative government—is profoundly threatened by the computer and the new media technologies. Making peace with the technology does not mean that the American democratic experience has to be scrubbed. On the contrary, what the new order does is offer an opportunity for the democratic system to *evolve* and improve. To dispel voter apathy; to jettison the perils of special interests; to involve the citizen to an extent never before believed possible are truly worthy goals. The ability to vote on public policy while snuggled under an electric blanket or munching on corn chips does not demean the system. On the contrary, the system can be enhanced and the American tradition honored.

American democracy is not a museum piece—a sculpture that was created in the eighteenth century to be admired, frozen in time. It is a dynamic, forever evolving mechanism insuring popular rule. While the names are the same, all the well-established institutions have changed since their inception. A presidential election is hardly what it was at the beginning. Not only did Washington have no opposition, but only four of the states allowed free white males to vote for electors. The remaining seven selected electors at conventions and legislative caucuses. Needless to say, the world of direct mail, political consultants, and TV ads was not even imaginable. The same could be said for the incredible changes in Congress and in state and local governments. The political structure that was then and is now is the same in name only. Institutions change.

The new technology makes direct democracy possible, indeed probable. As with all institutional change, this one will seep slowly into the system. It will not arrive with the crack of thunder or a new Constitutional Convention. The first video votes will be cast at the most local level. Even at that, the electronic plebiscites will be little more than public opinion samples. But gradually, legal authority will creep into the new system of polling. The power of law will replace the moral authority of public opinion. Politics as we know it will have been transformed. Call it video democracy.

What is proposed here is to merge the spirit of ancient Athens with the techologies of the twenty-first century—Pericles with digital transmission. Direct democracy can and should have a rebirth. At the very least, communities wired for interactive cable should experiment with direct democracy. In the pages that follow it will be argued that such experimentation is entirely consistent with the American political tradition and with the forces of history. The new democracy should move from the pages of scholarship to the stage of everyday politics. Only in that context can both the system and the technology be appropriately evaluated.

The tools already exist to personalize, indeed democratize, the system as never before. Technology cannot be denied; the future cannot be buried. Failure to adapt to the new order invites political disaster.

Safeguards must be established to retain the multitude of institutional structures so essential to the nation. For reasons to be explained later, video democracy will probably not threaten the existence of Congress and state legislatures; it would be unwise to tamper with institutions which work. Yet on a local level, the video revolution can bring the benefits of citizen participation to a summit never achieved in this nation. An experiment in direct democracy is necessary. Try the technology on for size. It may stimulate popular participation. It may make government more responsive. It may work.

The time is here to make peace with the new technology. It is already in our homes. If untamed, it could devour some excellent political institutions. If domesticated, it could make the democratic experience leap from the civics text to real life.

1

THE TALKING TUBE

COLUMBUS, OHIO IS to Madison Avenue what the peak of a bell-shaped curve is to statisticians. Demographically Columbus is the midline of Middle America. It is the town where new wonders of the laundry room are first tested and where American business finds out which bathroom tissue is most squeezable. Columbus is Test Market City U.S.A. And so it's only fitting that the Ohio capital has also been the test market for the hardware of the video revolution.

Don't be deceived by Columbus's reputation for averageness. The town is unique in several respects. It is, certainly, the only city west of the Hudson where New York Yankee caps are worn with pride, a testament to the fact that George Steinbrenner retains his top farm club there. Columbus is also the first city in the country where the word *cube* was spelled with a *Q*.

QUBE is the trade name Warner-Amex Communications coined for its two-way or interactive television operation in Columbus. Two-way means just that—the viewer is not merely a receiver of a broadcast, but can also "talk back" to the set and have his responses picked up, recorded, and tabulated by the cable company. QUBE is important because it was the first such operation. Its twenty-four thousand subscribers are the white rats of a new technology.

Warner-Amex did not stop with Columbus. Interactive systems were built in Cincinnati, Dallas, Houston, and Pittsburgh, though the latter station was later sold. Other companies have experimented with interactive technology. In the early 1980s, AT&T and CBS placed terminals in two-hundred homes in Ridgewood, New Jersey. Subscribers could access eight to ten thousand pages of information from their terminals. Among the benefits afforded those participating in the AT&T experiment was the ability to receive stories from several newspapers and to shop electronically in twenty stores. Other companies have dabbled in interactive TV in markets as far apart as San Diego and Ft. Lauderdale. Numerous small communities have experimented with two-way TV.

The word *experiment* is used because, as of this writing, no one has made money from two-way TV. Cable franchisers used to say the bonanza was just a silicon chip away. But no more. Interactive cable has fallen on difficult times. The wild predictions of the late 1970s have given way to a very sober assessment of the two-way cable marketplace.

For $40 a month in South Florida, one can become a "Viewtron" subscriber. And if one accepts the heavy promotion of this two-way TV system, "Viewtron" is all things to all people. It is the ultimate resource for the teenager struggling with homework, the businessman working on a deal, and the housewife battling the traffic at the local shopping center. "Viewtron," the advertising seems to imply, is the happy robot. It does your shopping, banking, and research, and then, when the chores are completed, becomes the home fun center offering games and entertainment. But where does "Viewtron" go to find new subscribers? It goes to the conventional VHF TV stations, because the viewers are still watching over-the-air TV.

By the mid-1980s, few companies wanted to acquire cable franchises that would be constructed to two-way specifications. This was a dramatic about-face, indeed, from the heady atmosphere of only a few years before. What happened?

Lesson one of American business is that no one wants to be second to jump onto a technological bandwagon, expecially a technology which promises to have an electronic hand on the family checkbook. The new technology promised to be a permanent fixture in every household. It would be better than an appliance—it would be a utility, like water, electricity, and the telephone. But the two-way cable would be practical because it provided essential services *and* entertainment. The device which served up twenty-four-hour-sports would also be the burglar alarm; what brought porn flicks into the bedroom would also monitor the gas meter; what gave pay-for-view movies would also deliver the morning paper (electronically, of course). The list went on. As endless were the possibilities of entertainment programming, so was the list for in-home services. Shopping, banking, schooling, communicating all would be housed in the same terminal that sheltered Jane Fonda's work-out and Michael Jackson's concert tour.

America, it seemed to the cable people, had two insatiable appetites—one for home entertainment and one for convenience. The same American ingenuity that brought the world drive-thru hamburgers, machine banking, and microwave tacos would now merge entertainment and convenience. The future of interactive cable seemed limitless and abundant.

The gold rush of interactive cable was fueled by some too-good-to-be-true numbers, although some may yet become reality. In an article extolling buying stocks via the home computer, the *New Yorker* predicted that half of all households will have home computers by 1993, and half of them will be interactive.[1] Despite the enormous capital expense, two-way cable, some experts said, would sweep the country. By the end of the 1980s, they said, thirty to forty-five million homes would have two-way capability. In turn, a new industry would be born to service the interactive homes. Those who think about such things predicted that the interactive market would be worth $10 to $16 billion dollars a year by the end of its first decade.[2]

The two-way system has a name. Videotex. Simply, it means there is a mechanism in the home for transmitting messages back to a central computer, usually the computer operated by the cable company. The user can summon an encyclopedic amount of information, from airline schedules to the menu at the local Chinese restaurant, and then respond to the information by informing the computer that he wants to fly to Buffalo or that he wants mou sou pork with extra pancakes. Certain companies saw an obvious dovetailing of their resources with the videotex technology. The Dow Jones Corporation, for example, financed videotex experiments with the stated purpose of selling stock information. Newspapers saw a bountiful future in videotex as a cheap way of delivering both news and, more importantly, classified advertising. No wonder that Knight-Ridder, the publishing giant, outfitted five thousand Florida homes with videotex at an expense of $26 million.[3]

The illusion of instant corporate success was fueled by some powerful demographics. A Knight-Ridder survey predicted that the typical videotex household would be headed by a male aged twenty-five to forty-nine; the household would have an income of over $35,000 and would be populated by people wanting convenience—so-called "action oriented" people who have the purchasing power to buy what they want. The videotex concept was Madison Avenue in neon—reaching the man watching NFL football, attending the opera and carrying an American Express card all at the same time. Videotex was to be the consumer express of the eighties. Any company failing to hop aboard was a fool. Woe to the company coming in second.

Like many sure things, the early videotex experiments were mired in miscalculation. The industry foundered on optimism.

First, the American cable industry confused acceptance of the basic product with a desire for a new and different future product. By 1983, cable was adding 400,000 new subscribers a month.[4] And people were watching. A survey in wired Tulsa showed that 56 percent watched network prime-time television compared to 83 percent nationwide.[5] Another poll of two thousand cable subscribers showed that 37 percent watched network, 36 percent cable, 18 percent had no preference and 9 percent watched independent or Public Broadcasting systems.[6] Apparently, the once lordly networks were on the run. It was estimated that the networks would command a mere 65 percent of the prime-time audience in 1990, compared to 91 percent in 1977-78.[7]

The research firm of Yankelovich, Skelly & White predicted that "ABC, CBS and NBC will be the *Life, Look* and *Saturday Evening Post* of the future." Like radio thirty years previously, the networks would now be the victims of mass technological change.

In a sense, the cable boom is based more on faith in tomorrow than on solid financial data today. Cable operators are only too aware of the enormous cost of wiring a community. A city like Baltimore with 300,000 households (many of them indigent) is expected to cost over $100 million to wire for cable. The capital expense, $80,000 per mile to cable underground and $10,000 above ground, is staggering. And the franchise fee paid to local government often carries no relationship to profit. The programming people have fared even worse than the cable operators. CBS lost $50 million on its cultural channel before shutting down the service. ABC, Westinghouse, and Viacom have spent over $100 million on programming which has yet to profit. To date, the most likely cable survivors are Cable News Network, MTV (music video) the Christian Broadcasting Network, and Nickelodeon (children's programming).[8] What they share is a philosophy of targeting a very specific audience.

Why has corporate America bled its stockholders to buy cable systems? Profit margins are thin. Lucky is the cable company signing up half of the potential customers in a given market area.

But research says that the average American family spends nearly seven hours a day with eyes riveted to the tube and only fourteen minutes a day conversing with each other. Futurists have coined the word "vidiots" to describe this average family. Psychologists have long toyed with the theory that people are becoming passively dependent on the TV for most human intercourse, insulated from any idea or experience not safely prepackaged for home consumption. And the cable companies were most eager to deliver those packages, for a price, of course, to those hungry consumers.

In media-talk the word is narrowcasting. With upwards of one-hundred channels, programmers can talk to specific groups with specific interests. Where over-the-air, network broadcasting prospered on the premise of mass marketing, cable grew on the theory of specialized programming. Some observers, like Dean George Gerbner of the University of Pennsylvania's Annenberg School of Communications, hailed cable as "a transformation of our world similar to the one brought about by the printing press."[9] Others, like *New York Times* humorist Russell Baker, spoofed cable, saying it was attempting to "Divide among 180 channels material already inadequate for 12."[10] A writer for *Fortune* wondered about "whole channels devoted exclusively to rock 'n' roll, and others to soap operas, game shows, or shows about such exotica as Ukranian shoemaking, Bavarian hops growing, sex therapy for newlyweds."[11]

In just one decade, from the mid-1970s to the mid-1980s, America whizzed through the first generation of cable. Cable, of course, had been around since the late 1940s when an appliance dealer in rural Pennsylvania figured out that he could bring TV to backwoods communities by erecting mountain-top antennas and linking the homes to the antennas by cable. The idea was to sell more televisions.

But contemporary cable was truly born in the mid-1970s, when RCA launched its first communications satellite, SATCOM I. In 1975, Home Box Office began sending movies to cable subscribers by satellite. Until that time cable was saddled by an FCC regulation prohibiting cable operators from bringing distant signals into the one-hundred largest TV markets. Once that regulation was deleted and the era of "unfettered competition" began, the cable industry soared as high as its satellites.

So great were the expectations of profits that it was only a matter of time before a cable company president went to jail for bribing a local official in an effort to secure a franchise. In the largest markets it is customary to spend millions for the right to wire a city.

While the first few years of interactive cable have been less than auspicious for cable's stockholders, the same cannot be said for all interactive technology. The moderate success of videotex companies, such as CompuServe, are reminders that interactive technology *can* find a market.

This corporation, also Columbus, Ohio-based, began videotex service in 1979. Five years later CompuServe had 128,000 subscribers. CompuServe differs from interactive cable in that it does not offer studio video. The system solely involves computers talking to computers. It offers subscribers the ability to access eight-hundred features from a tree-structured menu.[12] Technically, CompuServe is compatible with most home computers. The subscriber not only can retrieve information on finance, world and local news, transportation schedules, and the like, but also communicate with other subscribers through electronic mail. Indeed, the CompuServe subscriber can access any one of several newspapers and with a printer get a hard copy of a story that is not available at the hometown newstand.

The fact is that videotex's natural market is the business community, where companies need quick, easy, no frills information and are willing to pay for that service. It is predicted that electronic or E-mail will soon grow into a $2- to $3-billion-dollar-a-year industry.[13] Two dozen firms are currently competing for the E-mail dollar. So far they are hemorrhaging red ink, but their belief is that once a company has adopted E-mail, the service will never be dropped.[14]

CompuServe has also attempted to stake out the consumer market. The company offers a service called "the electronic mall," which is on-line twenty-four hours a day, seven days a week. Stores such as Sears, Bloomingdale's, and I-Magnin sell products over the computer hook-up. A customer can ask merchants questions and place orders without leaving the living room sofa.[15]

The videotex system of CompuServe and its competitors is not entirely analogous to interactive cable. What videotex lacks is a studio picture. Yet it is conditioning people to use their home computers interactively. Only a small adaptation by viewers is needed to go from videotex to true interactive cable. Once people learn to accept videotex they will welcome interactive cable. To that extent, videotex is not a rival of cable, but a companion technology.

Perhaps it is worthwhile to pause here for a semantic footnote. "Cable" is not necessarily cable. There is both a historic definition of cable and a generic one. Historically, cable TV, specifically interactive cable TV, is the two-way transmission of images and messages between a TV studio and data base and the home TV receiver/computer. To date, the sole provider of such services has been the cable industry. These are the same companies that had previously provided traditional one-way cable TV, a technology concerned only with entertainment. Slowly, new technologies are evolving which can both send and receive messages and images. In time the old cable companies will not have a monopoly on the interactive video market.

The greatest challenge to interactive cable comes from AT&T. Its system, dubbed Integrated Services Digital Network (or ISDN), uses phone lines rather than cable TV lines. As envisioned by AT&T the phone lines of the future will be quite different from contemporary lines. The central innovation is fiber optics. Fiber optics is the ability to use lasers to send pulses of light representing digital bits of information over strands of ultra-pure glass.[16] In tech talk the new AT&T system will be able to send 1.7 gigabits per second. The entire *Encyclopedia Britannica* could be transmitted in two seconds, as could 169,344 simultaneous conversations.[17]

Until the advent of the AT&T system, telephone lines transmitted voices in waves of electricity or analog form. The new ISDN system utilizes digital technology, codes using ones and zeroes which can be read by computers. What the fiber-optic/digital technologies mean for the future is this: The telephone will shortly be far more than a conversation piece. It will be a multi-media channel capable of transmitting voice, data, images, and video.[18]

Yes, it is futuristic. And yes, it will be years before every home can take advantage of ISDN technology. Cable still retains its monopoly as interactive television, but that is destined to change. The picture phone, which was a World's Fair toy, may well be revived. ISDN technology can do that and more. Whether the various phone companies adopting ISDN will open studios for the production and presentation of information and entertainment is not known. The decision to become an alternative television system might well depend upon the financial success of interactive cable TV.

For want of a better word—and probably none exists—the word *cable* is used throughout this book in both the historic and generic sense. Systems now in place, such as QUBE, are traditional cable systems. However, it is not the intent to say that video democracy must be restricted to cable TV. Clearly, any studio-to-home interactive system, whether it is ISDN or a still newer technology, is capable of carrying two-way political messages. In that sense, the word *cable* is used to denote any studio-to-home interactive technology.

There are 6,600 cable systems in the United States, serving 18,500 communities.[19] They reach 37.3 million households, estimated to include 104 million people. Fewer than half of the nation's TV households, 43.7 percent, have cable. Only a fraction have interactive cable.[20]

Cable remains, as it began, a rural-suburban phenomenon. If one looks at the fifty top cable cities in terms of household penetration, only San Diego, Honolulu, and Hartford-New Haven can be called major markets.[21] Cable's greatest penetration is most often in communities distant from big city broadcast TV. San Angelo, San Luis Obispo, Parkersburg, Laredo, Marquette, Clarksburg, Odessa, Johnstown, Beckley, and Yuma comprise the list of the top ten cable markets. While New York can boast 2 million cable households, that translates into only a 33-percent penetration rate. Cable's penetration in Los Angeles is lower than in New York and a mere 22 percent of TV households in Chicago are hooked up.[22]

Nevertheless, cable is a growth industry. In mid-1985, sixteen hundred franchises had been awarded, but not built. Most are one-way, with a minimum of twenty channels. Even though the cost of laying cable can be extraordinarily expensive, especially in central cities when cable must be placed underground, companies continue to pursue franchises because of cable's ultimate promise. No network executive can deny that cable is steadily eroding the national prime-time audience. Yet the costs of producing and buying programming and obtaining the franchise are so enormous that the cable gold mine has been tapped by relatively few companies.

Before America was able to digest one-way cable, the race to wire the country for interactive cable began. Cable companies like Warner-Amex weren't stupid. They were competitive. The competition the cable companies and their de facto allies, the newspapers, feared most came from AT&T. The bottom-line fact is that Ma Bell has squatters' rights. She is already *in* the home. In theory, an AT&T videotex system could become the industry standard. True, the phone company would have to upgrade its system to make it compatible with a computer, but that issue is largely technical. Cable, where it exists, has forty-five thousand times the capacity of phone wire. The battle is still going on. Both the phone company and the cable industry accept as gospel that only one system will prevail. Will it be cable—with its marriage of the computer and the TV, or an advanced space-age telephone, which combines home computer terminal and central data base?

To complicate matters further, more than $300 million has already been spent by Western European and Japanese governments to develop a videotex system. Would both the American phone system and American cable companies lose out to foreign competition? In the early 1970s, for example, the British sought to provide video subtitles for the hearing impaired. They developed a teletext system or what was dubbed CEEFAX (for "see facts"). CEEFAX went on the air in

September 1974. This one-way textual service was sent out over the air and the viewer had to take whatever was sent at the speed it was sent. CEEFAX was essentially printed radio with travel reports, spot news, sports, and weather. Airports, pubs, restaurants, and other public places were the primary markets for the teletext system. The significance of CEEFAX was that it was a first step for the British in a successful effort to take the lead in interactive video.

In 1979, the British Post Office launched PRESTEL, a full-fledged videotex system. The ingredients were a TV, a telephone, and a small calculator-sized keypad. PRESTEL could do it all: It could help with tax problems, mortgage calculations, and legal advice. PRESTEL could store a quarter of a million pages of information and keep all of it instantly available to several hundred callers at once.

"Our aim is to provide a cheap and universal means of electronic publishing, available to all, a new medium of communication, comparable in scale to radio, television and the press," said Alex Reid, the head of the PRESTEL Division of the British Post Office shortly after the videotex system was inaugurated.

In recent years, PRESTEL introduced digital reproduction of photographic images. This technology has been widely used by the real estate industry to picture listings.[23]

PRESTEL's corporate managers claim to have sold 1,000 sets a month in 1983, double the 1982 volume.[24] In all, some 700 financial firms, government institutions, publishers, and travel agencies participate in PRESTEL.[25] At-home shopping and banking are also part of the PRESTEL package. In a phrase, PRESTEL is called the "premier videotex product."[26]

But here in the United States the threat to cable is not from PRESTEL and similar technologies. From the perspective of the cable industry, the cruelest cut of all comes from other providers of home television entertainment. They are known in the business by their initials: MDS; STV; LPTV, and DBS. These providers of programming are leeches to the cable industry. They don't pay franchise fees, don't pay to lay cable underground or on telephone poles, and often don't pay for programming. These new technologies are stealing viewers who, the cable operators claim, ought to belong to them:

—MDS: Multipoint distribution service—an over-the-air, line-of-sight broadcasting of a single channel of video to microwave subscribers with special receivers.

—STV: Subscription television—a single-channel video broadcast service available on VHF or UHF channels with scrambled signals which can be seen with a decoding receiver.

—LPTV: Low-power television—a single-channel video which broadcasts to subscribers in a small geographic area.

—DBS: Direct-broadcast satellite—several video channels are offered to those with special rooftop, dish antenna; either subscription or advertiser supported.[27]

It is not the DBS service, but the dish itself which is so noxious to the cable companies. Perhaps they could live with the DBS providers, a detente among the earth stations. But the dish—the dish threatens the few profitable aspects of cable. Anyone owning a dish can pick up between 60 and 150 channels, if programs aren't scrambled. To the cable industry it is piracy. To the dish manufacturers it is big business. By the end of 1984, there were between 400,000 and 600,000 direct broadcast satellite dishes in use. These backyard space stations were growing at the astounding rate of 300 percent per year.[28]

So the cable industry found itself assaulted from all sides. Before the beleaguered industry could begin to turn the anticipated profits and pay off the enormous debt for wiring America, a host of competitors jumped into the arena. Who will entertain America? Will it be CATV, MDS, STV, LPTV, or DBS—with its unwanted offspring, the non-subscription backyard earth station? And how about VHF and UHF television? The medium that changed American life as nothing since the harnessing of electricity is still around. Some viewers still might opt for free, over-the-air broadcast television.

The advantage cable has over all these new video technologies (including the video tape recorder) is the capacity to be interactive, to merge television with the transmission of information between computers. Sure, someday someone will invent an inexpensive way for the home viewer to transmit up to a satellite and then back down to a central computer. But that day has not arrived. Thank goodness, says the cable industry.

The decision for cable to rush into interactive TV, long before the nation had yet digested one-way cable, is not as ludicrous as one might think. It was an end run. It was an attempt to score with the TV consumer by doing something the competing technologies could not—allowing the viewer to talk back to the set.

It would be easy to blame the cable industry's moving too fast on interactive cable and then retreating just as fast, on poor judgment and a lousy sense of the marketplace. After all, few can fully appreciate a new technology at its inception. Victorians thought the telephone would be a medium of entertainment; broadcasting pioneer David Sarnoff believed radio's best use would be to bring the concert hall to rural America; newspaper editors predicted TV would never be an instrument of news; and computer scientists in the 1950s saw no need for the devices outside the laboratory.

Unable to compete on an equal basis by providing one-way entertainment programming, cable rushed into the two-way battle with AT&T and foreign competition. It has been an expensive war. It costs a cable company about $600 to outfit a home for interactive TV. At a minimum, a home needs a modulator, an amplifier, and several sophisticated electronic devices in order to have the capability of responding to the TV. On a more advanced level, the TV is not just a polling device, but a home computer. To compete effectively with the phone company and foreign products, the domestic cable industry had to merge its system with the computer fully. The results have been far from spectacular. As one expert said: There was no product and no demand. Or was there no demand and no product.

It turns out that the American viewer did not want to be polled on what the first baby born on QUBE Day in Columbus should be named. People in New Jersey did not want to read the *Los Angeles Times* while the computer meter was ticking. People did not want to shop at home; they wanted to touch and see the product.

In the mid-1980s television remains what it always was—entertainment. The cable industry ran headlong into the interactive business because it felt it was squeezed by the phone company on one side and new video technologies on the other. The people wanted "General Hospital" and a Prince concert, not tele-banking and a living room supermarket.

They have not had the programming to complement either their vision or their technology. But cable has seen the future—and that future belonged to the competition unless they moved first.

Notes

1. "Videotex," *New Yorker* 59 (July 8, 1983): 26.

2. Eric Pace, "Videotex: Luring Advertisers," *New York Times*, October 14, 1982.

3. Peter Kaplan, "The Inevitable Machine," *Esquire* 110 (October 1983): 127.

4. "The Rush to Cable Is Now Turning Into a Retreat," *Business Week*, no. 2812 (October 17, 1983): 142.

5. "Is Cable TV Losing Its Luster?" *U.S. News and World Report*, November 22, 1982, 72.

6. "Cable Connects with Viewers,"*USA Today*, December 3, 1984, D-1.

7. Eric Gelman, "The Video Revolution," *Newsweek* 104, no. 6 (August 6, 1984): 56.

8. "The Rush to Cable," 135.

9. Harry Waters, "Cable TV: Coming of Age," *Newsweek* 98, no. 8 (August 24, 1981): 49.

10. Ibid., 46.

11. Peter W. Bernstein, "Television's Expanding World," *Fortune* 99, no. 13 (July 2, 1979): 69.

12. Mary Tonne Schaefer, "Videotex in the United States," *Information Retrieval & Library Automation* 20, no. 2 (July 1984): 2.

13. Kevin Anderson, "Electronic Mail in Survival Fight," *USA Today*, March 11, 1985, B-1.

14. Ibid., B-2.

15. Schaefer, "Videotex," 2.

16. William D. Marbach and William J. Cook, "The Revolution in Digitech," *Newsweek* 105, no. 11 (March 18, 1985): 49.

17. Ibid.

18. Andrew Pollack, "Enhancing Phone Lines," *New York Times*, March 21, 1985, D-2.

19. *Broadcasting/Cablecasting Yearbook* 1985 (Washington, D.C.: Broadcasting Publications, Inc.): D-3.

20. Ibid.

21. Ibid., D-343.

22. Ibid.

23. Paul Hurly, "The Promises and Perils of Videotex," *The Futurist*, no. 2 (April 1985): 10.

24. Mary Tonne Schaefer, "Quo Vadis Videotex?" *Information Retrieval & Library Automation* 19, no. 12 (May 1984): 4.

25. Ibid.

26. Ibid.

27. Ernest Holsendolph, "Tougher Times for Cable TV," *New York Times,* July 11, 1982, F-24.

28. Society for Private and Commercial Earth Stations (SPACE), 709 Pendleton Street, Alexandria, VA 22314.

2

BABES IN QUBELAND

THE CABLE INDUSTRY is, indeed, in a period of transition—from where and to where is not at all clear. In the late seventies and early eighties cable pursued the interactive technology. Communities asked for interactive systems and cable was more than anxious to oblige. Then, realizing the enormous cost of a two-way system and the less than overwhelming consumer demand, cable backed off from the promise of a videotex tomorrow. Experiments would continue, but the wholesale wiring of America with two-way TV would be put on hold.

Simply put, by the mid-1980s two-way cable was backsliding. One could not call it wholesale retreat, since many still trumpeted the technology. Ambivalent retreat might best describe the attitude of cable companies. In Milwaukee, for example, Warner-Amex deferred construction of the interactive portion of the system. Cox Cable projects in Omaha and Tucson also had two-way systems placed on hold. In South Florida, Miami Cablevision received permission to eliminate the franchise requirement for interaction. Even some existing systems, most notably several operated by Warner-Amex, had their two-way technology cut back or scrapped.

But why? There are two answers, says Michael Doyle, general manager of Comsat of Maryland, the nation's 13th largest cable system located in suburban Baltimore. Two-way cable costs too much and the product is scarce. Nevertheless, promises Doyle, "Interactive is definitely the wave of the future."

Doyle belongs to the optimists. The cable industry has no shortage of those whose belief in interactive remains firm. Yet there is an equally large segment of the industry which contends that cable jumped far ahead of itself and the marketplace when it began wiring for two-way TV. One noted executive in the industry argues that the promotion of interactive cable was little more than a public relations stunt "in order to get things through the FCC. Two-way franchising has been a tool and a promotional gimmick for twelve years."[1]

The pessimists can point to some staggering failures in recent years of standard one-way cable. In September 1982, CBS's ambitious cultural cable service folded after only 11 months of operation and a $30 million loss. The ABC-Westinghouse Satellite News Channel was born in 1982 and died in the fall of 1983, losing an estimated $60 million.[2] Such numbers would be sobering to the most vocal boosters.

Realistically, most cable systems will probably opt to enter the interactive sphere gradually. While there will undoubtedly continue to be experimentation and technical development of interactive TV, to those in corporate board rooms, prudence dictates a cautious approach. The first step towards universal acceptance of interactive TV will likely be the adoption of electronically addressable converter boxes. That is the device which registers pay-per-view selections. Cable operators call it an impulse box, because it enables viewers to make a last minute decision on choosing entertainment programming, as opposed to phoning the cable company to request a particular movie or show.

And yet there is something very special about interactive cable; something that separates cable from its communications competitors.

What the cable industry has failed to see is that interactive TV is its only option. The phone company system can probably deliver two-way communication between terminals less expensively than cable. For example, one technology is called Local Area Data Transport (LADT). It makes at-home shopping, banking, and communication possible by sending data over existing phone lines through packet switching. The technology allows users to bundle information from several customers which is then sent over a single digital phone line. In essence, it is like videotex, computer talking to computer. It provides information, but it is not television. Then there are the competing video technologies, which offer an endless list of programming options. Over the long term it is less expensive to buy a dish to pick up entertainment than to pay $40 a month for cable. These technologies provide television, but not for entertainment.

Consumers and the industry itself have soured on two-way TV. Each is to blame. Neither has realized the long-term potential of the technology; the industry gave consumers an interactive version of the "Dating Game" and consumers gave the industry little enthusiasm for the "new" product.

Let's take a look at QUBE, the original. Basically, QUBE is plain, old, familiar cable TV. The system carries over-the-air VHF channels, cable channels, and locally operated two-way channels. You see what you pay for, and monthly TV bills can run as high as $150. A championship prize fight might cost a consumer more than the basic monthly fee. X-rated films might cost even more. In fact, QUBE's mostly white and mostly middle class audience has continually shelled out a disproportionate share of its TV budget for soft-porn. Speculating on the future of "interactive" X-rated broadcasts is somewhat beyond the scope of this book. Parenthetically, however, a woman who described herself as elderly and on the prudish side wrote a local Columbus newspaper that she was outraged because QUBE had billed her for watching *Captain Lust* ten times. Such unintentional computer error is understandable, since one out of every three QUBE subscribers did, in fact, punch the button for "Captain Lust" at least once on the computerized keypad alongside the TV set.

Perhaps it is grossly unfair to judge interactive TV by the QUBE experience. The system is not integrated with a vast computer system. The viewer has only five response buttons, not an entire keyboard. The entertainment programming has remained fairly traditional TV, but with a gimmick. But because it is the patriarch of interactive cable, QUBE is a useful illustration—an example of the good, the bad, and the potential of two-way cable. This is not to say that the Warner-Amex system is any better or its motives any more altruistic than those of many other cable systems. It must be remembered that the QUBE system is primitive, even by today's technology. Moreover, it was never designed as a political vehicle. First, the purpose of QUBE was to see if it would work; second, to see if the product could attract customers. The answer to the first question is "yes" and to the second, "we're still not sure."

As time passes, new interactive systems, indeed, new technologies, will arise. QUBE was the first and has a history. For that reason alone it merits a closer look, a glimpse at a fictional-sounding but very real example, an innovation on the traditional talk-show format that might be better defined as George Gallup does Phil Donahue.

The prime vehicle for "QUBE" programming in Columbus has been a talk show called "Columbus Alive." All that separates it from hundreds of TV talk shows through the country is its use of interactive technology. The set, issues and chit chat are virtually indistinguishable from standard TV talk. As with most of the talk show genre, Columbus Alive" is designed to promote causes, entertain and most often sell a new book. Only when the talk show host asks viewers to "touch-in"—the phrase used on all "QUBE" shows instructing the viewers to depress keypad buttons—does "Columbus Alive" take on a special dimension. One show asked viewers to select eligible bachelors. At various times viewers have voted on what a newborn girl should be named—the choice was Sophia Lynn Elizabeth; who should be on the cover of *US* magazine—the pick was the Incredible Hulk; what color should the city's transit buses be painted—the selection was a white body with orange and brown trim. Questions on abortion, homosexuality, traffic control, and drugs are staples of the multiple-choice format. The results of the vote are immediately tabulated and projected on the TV screen in percentages. Percentages alone do not make for good science or good polling, but Warner-Amex refuses to give out actual numbers.

In addition to "Columbus Alive," the two-way TV format is used by a game show called (what else?) "The Magic Touch." There is no studio contestant, but QUBE's computer scores viewer responses to trivia questions and eventually, by elimination, selects a champion from the home audience. Still another show calls upon the viewers to interact with Mr. QUBEsumer and through the push button system comment on failings of particular products.

Off camera, one talk show host calls the QUBE response system "a point of departure for discussion rather than a way of settling an issue." The TV host is quick to note that QUBE greatly oversimplifies the issues, reducing everything to a multiple choice question. Less generous is Dr. Sharon Dunwoody, who teaches research methods at the Ohio State University School of Journalism. "QUBE is a grave misuse of survey technique. They say it is not a scientific survey, yet they treat it like it is. Your average American will misunderstand this. They [Warner-Amex] may say 80 percent respond in a certain way. Eighty percent of what? You never know."[3]

"QUBE is the perfect example of technology outstripping the imagination that created it," commented Jeff Borden, TV critic for the *Columbus Dispatch*. "It hasn't done one significant thing since I've been watching it."[4] As one regular viewer put it, in six months the only thing worth voting on was a tanning contest.

It is difficult to assess QUBE on the basis of its entertainment programming. The purpose of interactive TV, at least for the cable companies, is economic, not emotional and certainly not cerebral. It is seen by proponents as the ultimate marketing device. Marketing experts know that many sales are lost because the consumer has time to consider the wisdom of a particular purchase. That is not the case with two-way TV. The sales pitch and the consumer decision to buy or not to buy are virtually simultaneous. The gap between message and decision is eliminated. Once motivated, all the consumer has to do is "touch in."

Warner-Amex has experimented with so-called Qubits— commercials lasting up to two minutes and calling on the viewer to participate. The cable company also has so-called "informationals"—commercials running up to a half-hour which are sometimes passed off as entertainment. A major marketing asset of the cable system is that a sponsor's message can be directed to a particular household. For an advertiser, interactive cable has all the advantages of targeted direct mail and all the visual impact of TV. Moreover, the viewer can shop right in his living room. With systems slightly more sophisticated than QUBE, the viewer has to do no more than punch in his credit card number and say good-bye to shopping malls forever. Theoretically, cable enables the viewer to bring classified ads to life. So you want to buy a 1983 Pontiac? Use your keyboard to list the specifications—red, under $4,000, V-6 engine, two doors. Feed all your requirements into the computer and seconds later a listing of every available car meeting the specifications will appear on the home screen. There is no need to limit the market to one's home town. Anyone in the country with a two-way cable system could, in theory, plug into this new national marketplace. In terms of shopping at home, for now QUBE goes only so far as enabling viewers to order books. "If you would like to order one of these books, touch the corresponding buttons and the computer will gather you name and address." The computer knows exactly who's calling in.

Then the day arrived when retailers and cable companies said, "Eureka! We don't need this cumbersome and expensive computer system to sell products. Let's show the viewer a catalogue from Saks, Penneys, Sears, or General Motors and simply give him an 800 number to call and give his credit card number." One-way cable systems did not have to upgrade their systems to become a video marketplace. Several channels would be devoted to video shopping. These channels would broadcast more than conventional commercials. A salesperson would not be limited to a thirty-second spot. He would spend an hour discussing the merits of various Sears dryers and finally offer the phone number to call.

This system has been dubbed "soft" interactive. Soft, because the viewer is responding to a message, but there is no mechanism in the TV for making that response. Clearly, soft interactive is at some disadvantage to "hard" two-way TV. With a hard system, the viewer can call up a specific video catalogue and receive a particular sales pitch on a particular product. With the soft system, the viewer is limited to what is being peddled on the cable channel that day; the viewer has no choice. In addition, the viewer cannot punch his selection and credit card number directly into the home terminal—and presumably have his money automatically withdrawn from his bank account.

Yet the advantage of soft interactive is considerable. A soft interactive system costs a fraction of the amount it takes to wire and equip a hard interactive system. With the advent of soft interactive systems, the future of genuine two-way TV was further diminished.

In fairness to the cable industry, the economics have worked against the further expansion of two-way TV. If the primary mission of the two-way concept was to sell products more efficiently than old-fashioned TV advertising, then soft interactive functioned almost as well as hard interactive and at a far lower cost.

But there are many who see two-way TV as more than a marketing tool and more than a technique to beef up viewer interest in a talk show. The implications for government as it has always been practiced in the United States are profound. While economics may have stalled or delayed the eventual wiring of the nation into an interactive network, the issue presented by the technology is of enormous consequence.

Since two-way TV was first and foremost a marketing device, there has been little application to politics. But QUBE, to its credit, has taken some small steps to apply technology to local government. Upper Arlington, Ohio is what people are supposed to aspire to. The city's first name tells much of the story. It is richer, older, better educated, and on the very top of the charts in virtually every category of socioeconomic indicators. It is a community of 42,000 living in distinguished brick and shingle homes, where aluminum siding is considered an offense and crabgrass a blight on the neighborhood. The new city hall is across the street from a country club. A bulletin board in city hall carries announcements for aerobics classes, art league meetings, and something called creative play. None of these is exactly a burning urban issue.

Democratic thinkers proffer that a community the size of Upper Arlington is close to perfect. Citizens can feel involved and can know civic leaders personally, problems appear manageable, and the community is largely homogeneous. If one were to seek a community to experiment with direct democracy, Upper Arlington would be an excellent selection. Small communities promote democratic attitudes. Of course, the QUBE programming never intended to go so far as to change the mayor-council system. Therefore, the experience with two-way TV in Upper Arlington and neighboring communities is limited at best.

A profile of the Upper Arlington City Council begins and ends with the word Republican. Included on the council is an advertising executive, a CPA, a corporate vice president, and an insurance executive. The city's mayor is the son-in-law of the state's former governor. Upper Arlington is also part of QUBEland. No one will ever dismiss this suburban Columbus community as Middle America— Upper America, maybe. Yet it is here in the very core of status quo suburbia that the new age of video politics dawned.

The issue was a planning study. A more mundane topic would be hard to conjure. But no one said political revolutions began with marching bands and mass demonstrations. Sometimes, as in this case, revolutions begin with zoning questions. On July 12, 1978, QUBE viewers in Upper Arlington (QUBE can narrowcast, that is, direct a signal only to the homes of residents of a particular community) were asked to vote for or against a planning study of the older portion of the city. Few thought of the vote as a historic experiment in direct democracy, but that was what it was. Since the local newspaper had run a series on the planning study prior to the telecast, many in the community were well informed. During the two-and-one-half-hour QUBE telecast, viewers got their fill of sewers, street lighting, and road paving. The actual vote was not binding on anyone, but it does not take a quantum leap of the imagination to see the day when local governmental bodies will be forced to abide by the results of video votes. When the televised explanation of the planning proposal ended, viewers were asked to "touch in." They did and turned thumbs down to the planning study. To a follow-up question, the viewers overwhelmingly approved the concept of using QUBE for public hearings.

James Waldsmith, editor of the *Upper Arlington News*, says the video vote—though it had no legal clout—did assure the ultimate rejection of the plan by city fathers. "No doubt about it," says Waldsmith, "it didn't really cause a change in the outcome, but it reinforced what was already heard in the public hearings."

Who knows how many Upper Arlington residents voted? QUBE does and it isn't telling. The percentages alone were sufficient to convince the city's elected leaders that public opinion was opposed to the plan. What occurred in Upper Arlington following the video vote on the planning study confirms the age-old adage that politicians will jump on anything that places them on the side appearing to represent the majority. From the moment Upper Arlington touched in, proponents of the planning study were on the defensive.

The future of America, especially local government, is seen in embryonic form in Upper Arlington and neighboring communities. Since the planning study vote, Upper Arlington politicos have had regular opportunities to appear on QUBE in a show called "Upper Arlington Plain Talk." The show does not have the blessing of Upper

Arlington officialdom. "Plain Talk" is produced by an ad hoc group of citizens with no formal connection to city government. In fact, Upper Arlington mayor Richard Moore calls the show "a waste of time."

"Any politician who bases opinions on QUBE polls and believes they have impact is a fool," says Moore. "QUBE won't tell you the number of people watching and I don't want to be part of it. There's no statistical validity to the QUBE vote.[5] Moore offers the hypothetical example of the family dog inadvertently stepping on the keypad as he makes his way toward a bowl of Alpo. Because there is no way, at present, to determine who or what is voting, the QUBE system must be taken as no more than an electronic show of hands.

Obviously, the success of any democratic system hinges on the accurate verification of eligible voters. Today there is theoretically no need physically to go to the polls and sign a card in the presence of an election judge before entering a voting booth. Automatic bank teller machines routinely hand out money after reading the magnetic tape on the back of a plastic card. Supermarket registers charge customers after scanning a bar code. The technology is readily available to distribute electronic voter registration cards which could be inserted and read by a home computer. The voter's identity and registration status could be verified in much the same way that banks verify money cards—with a code number and/or a thumbprint. There is no technical barrier standing in the way of living room democracy.

Upper Arlington is not the only Columbus suburb serviced by QUBE, nor is the affluent community the sole test of video voting. Many Upper Arlington residents trace their roots to Grandview Heights, a community just to the south. Grandview Heights is one of Columbus's original streetcar suburbs and probably hasn't changed much, save for the Mini Mart and pizza parlor, since the city was incorporated in 1931. The road sign calls Grandview Heights "The Friendly Little City," and by all accounts it fits the description, being both friendly and little. A mini-city only one square mile in size, Grandview Heights has its own government including police and fire departments. The 7,500 residents live either "uphill" in neat single family homes or "downhill" in apartments. There is an equal mix of white and blue collar. The city's main strip, Grandview Avenue, fell victim long ago to outer suburbia's shopping malls. What was once quite literally a grand avenue now has its share of boarded up store fronts and a theater which hasn't shown a movie in years. One reason residents do not patronize the old theater is that one third of Grandview Heights is wired for cable TV—not just cable but QUBE. Once a month Grandview Heights Mayor Lawrence Pierce along with members of the nonpartisan council and various department heads holds an electronic dialogue with constituents.

A TV critic could easily characterize Grandview Heights's show as a disaster. Community leaders, being amateurs, are frequently found looking at the wrong camera, gazing at the ceiling when responding to a viewer's telephone call, appearing pallid-faced from lack of make-up, and generally lacking in any TV presence. A more perceptive observer would call the show charming and genuine. Its unrehearsed quality and total absence of slickness is very much in keeping with the community itself: straightforward, proud, and a bit rough around the edges. "Meet the Press" it is not. Then again, no one from the Grandview Heights council is talking about nuclear proliferation or the prospects for a Middle East peace. Rather, the topics revolve around school taxes and teenagers hanging out on Grandview Avenue. As Mayor Pierce says, "Even I get bored during the shows." Stimulating TV it is not, but it is local and relevant.

As with Upper Arlington, the central question is, who is watching? At best, there are a couple of hundred community activists who tune into mayor Pierce's monthly sessions. Even though their opinions carry no legal weight, the council members and department heads take note of the percentages. Gallup isn't in Grandview Heights and QUBE is the only measure of public opinion available.

Moderator Pierce is keenly aware that he must navigate the show on the uncharted waters of electronic government. His mission is to keep partisanship off the cable. "I wouldn't think of using the show to try and persuade people to see things my way," says the mayor. "The show is meant for information and communication."

The twin problems of superficiality and snap judgments trouble Pierce. Democracy, even on the most local level, does require the contemplation of issues. A half hour of discussion and instant votes do not measure up well to the legacy of James Madison. Although Pierce is very much aware that the territory of video voting is mined with problems, he admits even he can be swayed by the percentages flashed on the QUBE screen. Politicians are by nature intoxicated by anything calling itself public opinion.

The politicians of Grandview Heights are caught in the eternal democratic bind—whether it is their job to represent or to follow. Roger Alban, a city councilman and school board member who has made several appearances on the QUBE tube, sees his role as representative: "Unless someone studies the issues like I do they just can't absorb it. QUBE can never take the place of the council. You need a political elite to run things. But the Grandview Community Forum does give us an opportunity to get feedback from the people. And I was elected to listen to the people."

The scientific sampling of public opinion has become a uniquely American art form. The nation is constantly polled on everything from its sexual tastes to its preferences in TV dinners; from what is wrong with pro football to what's right with the Council of Economic Advisors. What could be more perfectly American than to bring together the democratic instinct to count heads with the capitalistic passion to sell goods, services, and ideas. This love affair with the polls long ago affected the politician. By definition, the political animal needs to be liked, and more than liked, reelected. While aware of his legal responsibilities and often very knowledgeable about the facts, the politician filters everything through the sieve of public opinion.

What QUBE did for Columbus area politicians was place them in an impossible dilemma. Using unscientific polls, the politicians were left to vote in their legislative capacities on feedback which was dubious at best. Moveover, local politicians are ill-equipped to deal with the pressures of polls; people holding statewide or national office can more easily ignore polls. Their large and diverse constituencies have a built-in buffer to withstand the power of public opinion.

Additionally, true experiments in direct democracy should *not* attempt to graft a system of citizen participation onto a representative one. A real test of direct democracy must exist in a pure state. Legislative bodies, and even powerful executives, must give way, if the people are to be directly involved in the day-to-day process of government. But the QUBE public affairs programming placed local politicians in a situation in which they were neither fish nor fowl. They were part politician supposedly voting their consciences and part robot expressing the will of an unseen electorate.

While the politicians of Grandview Heights scrupulously avoid conflict, the same cannot be said for a third Columbus suburb tied into the Warner-Amex cable network. Gahanna is Grandview Heights thirty years ago. It is a young, growing suburb of 18,000. Eighty-five percent of the wage earners work outside the community. They live in Gahanna because it is a sanctuary from social conflict. The minority population hovers around 4 percent. The first bank robbery occurred in 1979; there has never been a murder and records say there has been only one suicide. In this expanding suburb, the major issues are zoning, annexation, and the development of an industrial park. Again, the issues are anything but profound.

Public sentiment runs high on the question of licenses for cats. Communities such as Gahanna, where violent crime and poverty are things to be read about in the downtown Columbus paper, have the luxury of contemplating cat licenses. It is a fortunate town indeed. Where Gahanna's QUBE talk show differs from the Grandview Heights show is not on the essentially local orientation, but in style. It is known for conflict, bickering, and partisanship.

Everyone concedes that Gahanna's televised town meeting is seen by a minority of its citizens. Everyone is aware that the votes are tallied in percentages and no one knows who is pushing buttons on the QUBE keypad. Still, the politicians believe in QUBE.

"Sure, we can be influenced by the QUBE votes," confides council member Judi Peterson, who happens to be a staunch opponent of feline registration. "What a vote does is help form a pattern of public opinion along with calls, letters and comments we hear on the street. I know people are paying attention to the discussions on QUBE. We've had shows where a vote at the beginning of the show is 60 to 40 percent against something and turned around to 40 to 60 by the end of the show." [6]

The Peterson rule is that it is best to confine QUBE votes to broad philosophical issues, such as choosing between more streets or more cops. Specifics, she says, are to be avoided. One would not ask the public to decide whether the new police cars should be Ford or General Motors products. But who is to decide what is appropriate for public debate and public decision? The Columbus communities serviced by QUBE have not figured out how to define the agenda.

To define the agenda is the ultimate challenge for proponents of direct democracy. While the national experience with direct citizen participation is limited, guideposts exist. There are two distinct types of issue voting—hard issue voting and easy issue voting.[7] Hard issue voting occurs when the voter carefully and deliberately weighs the costs and benefits of his vote. The voter votes for the candidate or for or against an issue because he stands to gain from the selection. The process requires conceptual skills. More interested, more motivated people are likely to be hard issue voters. Easy issue voting is what is often referred to as voting one's gut. An issue is easy when various positions can be reduced to symbols; it can be presented simply in non-technical terms; it deals with policy ends not means, and it has been on the political agenda for a long time.[8]

School prayer, abortion, and gun control are examples of easy issues. Most people have a gut response to those issues and are unlikely to be influenced by any amount of debate or deliberation. Direct democracy probably functions least effectively when citizens are presented with easy issues. The genius of interactive TV, which enables the citizen-voter to hear various sides of an issue, is meaningless when the agenda consists of easy issues.

On the contrary, when the agenda seeks to resolve hard issues, direct democracy is at its best. Few people have visceral reactions to allocating funds for filling potholes or licensing cats or any of thousands of issues entertained by local governments. The viability of direct democracy—at least in an experimental stage—rests on focusing attention on such hard issues. Communities that choose to use an interactive system to promote public participation would be advised to address those issues that require reason rather than emotion.

It is, of course, absurd for a governmental system to exclude certain volatile issues because people have preconceived opinions or because the issues are moral rather than pragmatic. After all, who would set the agenda? Yet for direct democracy to be viewed in the best possible light, the best instincts of the citizen voter must have a chance to emerge.

It is unfair and probably inaccurate to judge the merits of direct democracy from the experience of the three Columbus suburbs. Their attempts at electronic government were little more than talk television. But as forays into the world of mass public participation on issues, the shows are significant.

Warner-Amex feels good about the community forums. The company is satisfying a requirement to be involved in public affairs. Moreover, it is reinforcing the notion that interactive TV is just an extension of standard broadcasting and that the new technology does not encroach on privacy.

"Government tends to sit in an ivory tower," says John Schmuhl, QUBE's general manager. "It's frustrating as hell for the politicians. You can't get people involved. Go to town meetings and there's nobody there. We're trying to revitalize government. Politicians can use the results of our polls as another resource, another medium. We're bringing real events to television."[9]

Schmuhl has thought a great deal about the new technology: "I feel comfortable with the system. The only danger is if the polls become gospel. Sure, it's potential for Big Brother all over. But if people believe it's Big Brother, then no one will touch the buttons. If people fear the consequences, no one will tamper with the system. TV is a very compelling medium and we're trying to make it more than just a sterile viewing habit. QUBE is an active rather than a passive medium."

If nothing else, America is a nation of button pushers. We love gadgets, dials, digital displays, mechanical operations. Interactive TV brings a new toy into the home. The cable operators see the keyboard and television combination as a miniature shopping mall—just the right size to squeeze in the front door. But, as Schmuhl implies, if we fear the technology, it's doomed.

Others see the new technology as the key to opening up the political system as never before.

Notes

1. John Malone in Thomas Whiteside, "Onward and Upward With the Arts—Cable III," *The New Yorker*, vol. 61, (June 3, 1985): 101.

2. Ibid., 86, 92.

3. Steven Levy, "Speak Up Columbus," *Panorama* 2, no. 2 (February 1981): 58.

4. Ibid.

5. Richard Moore, Mayor, Upper Arlington, Ohio, personal interview, August 28, 1981.

6. Judi Peterson, Council member, Gahanna, Ohio, personal interview, August 27, 1981.

7. Edward Carmines and James Stimson, "The Two Faces of Issue Voting," *American Political Science Review* 74, no. 1 (March 1980): 75.

8. Ibid., 80.

9. John Schmuhl, general manager, Warner-Amex QUBE, Columbus, Ohio, personal interview, May 28, 1981.

3

A PHILOSOPHY REBORN

IT WAS APRIL 11, 1982. It was not the sort of day likely to jolt the memories of historians as a milestone in the evolution of democracy. It was an average kind of day until 11:30 that night.

At that time, the rather irreverent NBC show "Saturday Night Live" posed this question to viewers: "Shall Larry the Lobster Live or Die?" A phone number was given so viewers could register their feelings about Larry's fate. With his life hanging in the balance, thousands across the country paid fifty cents for an opportunity to express their opinions about Larry. Ultimately, Larry's life was spared by a telephone vote of 123,008 to 117,207.

Was the lobster vote political history? Perhaps, in a sense, it was. It was a national poll on an issue. It wasn't a traditional poll, a sampling of several hundred voters picked at random. It was asking everyone to participate, a form of direct democracy.

Two years later "Saturday Night Live" attempted another TV-telephone poll. This time, however, the issue was not life or death. It was the Democratic presidential nomination. Within ninety minutes more than a quarter million people voted. Initially, Jesse Jackson stormed into the lead. Once the heavy metal rock group Z Z Top had its name entered in the contest, Jackson and the other contenders faired poorly.

It was nonsense, of course, but it showed that Americans will respond to a TV poll even if the issue is admittedly absurd. The concept of voting, registering an opinion, is deeply ingrained in the American psyche. No one goes through an American education with its countless elections for class presidents, team captains, and hall monitors without internalizing the system.

America has always been primed for direct democracy. Structurally, the nation's institutions and much of the country's traditions have scorned direct democracy. By far, the majority of the Founding Fathers, those framers of the Constitution, valued property and order over liberty and social justice. And even if they were not worried about the rabble interfering with the affairs of government, the Founders were far too practical to believe that direct democracy could work. But the promise of a direct democracy survived, so that even contemporary commentators have recently written of a desire "to restore something of the vitality of the idea of democracy itself, to rediscover the originality of its challenge . . . and to reawaken the sense of excitement and fulfillment found in the ideal of direct participation."[1]

Jean-Jacques Rousseau, the patron saint of democratic ideals, had no illusions about the indirect system of government. He noted that the only time the English truly enjoyed political liberty was when they voted in parliamentary elections. The rest of the time the member of Parliament had the liberty and the citizen was left politically emasculated. No one's will, said Rousseau, could ever be represented by another.[2] The representative system is not democratic, Rousseau insisted.

Rousseau found his philosophic roots in the Athenian democracy between the sixth and fourth centuries B.C., where a form of direct democracy was practiced. He also was enamored with the "Alpine Democracy," where individuals came together to resolve communal problems.

Rousseau's model community was one in which each citizen participated directly in the day-to-day affairs of governing. In this way, said Rousseau, the individual acting freely for himself could remain at one with his community.[3] Though subject to much interpretation, Rousseau's famous concept of the "general will" appears to foretell a new entity; the very act of association creates a sovereign general will.

The French philosopher was practical enough to realize that large nation-states were hardly appropriate for direct democracy. His guidelines for the perfect democratic community were that it should be small, simple in manner, and egalitarian. In this environment, the individual acquires the feeling of freedom and belonging.

The United States was born large. Never could direct democracy be contemplated on a national sphere. Jefferson would take note of Rousseau when, at his first inaugural in 1801, he would differentiate between a republic and a democracy. The barriers to a direct democracy were so formidable that all speculation on direct citizen participation was consigned from the outset to the dreamers.

The one significant departure from the norm was the New England town meeting. It always seemed to function best when the town was no larger than three-thousand. The New England version of direct democracy was based on the following unwritten constitution: no citizen was excluded; all present were political equals; the meeting held final authority; officials were accountable; majority rule was unlimited; the focus was on local issues and the need for people to meet face to face.[4]

It is most revealing that QUBE calls its two-way public interest shows "community forum," "plain talk" and "town meeting."

Consciously or not, QUBE is reinventing the New England town meeting and rediscovering a political process which has fallen on years of neglect. One of the great ironies of political history is that a system of government which was terribly impractical years ago has been made totally feasible today through technology. America always has been too large geographically, too populous, and too heterogeneous for direct democracy to make a go of it.

But America has been downsized, to use an automotive term. What was unwieldy and impractical only a few years ago has become manageable and practical today. Video voting makes sense, if communities conform to Rousseau's overall dictum—that the communities are small.

Television made America homogenous. The networks unified the nation as nothing since the Revolution itself. Regional accents faded until folks from Alabama to Alaska began to sound like Walter Cronkite. Linguists called the speech pattern General American. Local culinary tastes gave way to the Big Mac, frozen pizza, and other foodstuffs which could be advertised nationally. Similarly, local political issues became adjuncts to national debates as politicians took their cues from network news.

From the fifties to the eighties America shed regional and local differences and became culturally unified as never before in its history. As the ad campaign for Holiday Inns states, wherever one travels, there are "no surprises." Television would take, and deserve, both the praise and the blame for the cultural amalgamation. TV blended a diverse and socially complex nation into a homogenized entity at the expense of precious regional diversity. The Johnny Carson monologue is a shared experience, as are space exploration, presidential elections, and Cabbage Patch dolls. Network TV was the great unifier. If a person missed a show or news story, he felt like an outcast in the factory lunchroom. Mass culture meant mass experience.

Then along came cable. Cable tailored its programming to small groups. Folk singers had their channels, as did homosexuals, aerobic dancers, and astronomers. In *The Third Wave*, futurist Alvin Toffler predicted the demassification of the media. He suggested that the media aimed at many small groups with a multitude of interests would lead to a collapse of consensus. The electorate, Toffler said, would break down into single issue groups—coalitions for specific purposes.[5] As yet, the networks still retain their grip on the nation's cultural pulse; the advent of Toffler's world will be delayed. But it is coming. Clearly, cable has introduced a new element into the political process. The networks no longer set every agenda and all the norms.

By and large, politicians have yet to grasp the significance of demassification. There have been exceptions. In 1982, Massachusetts reapportioned its Congressional districts. Rep. Barney Frank was placed in a district with another incumbent Rep. Margaret Heckler. Frank, a liberal Democrat, realized the only way he could win was to carry the town of Fall River, which had been represented by his opponent for sixteen years.

Forsaking the VHF network affiliates in Boston and Providence, Frank decided to concentrate his efforts on cable broadcasting. He would take the novel approach of reaching target voters on the cable, which was far less expensive than the traditional media campaign. Since a vast number of Fall River voters are first- and second-generation Portuguese immigrants, Frank purchased vast amounts of time on the Portuguese channel run by Whaling City Cable TV. The congressman used local people in thirty-second spots and a town meeting format for three half-hour shows. By election day Frank was better known in Fall River than his opponent and he defeated Heckler, the eight-term incumbent.[6]

Ed Dooley, vice-president of the National Cable Television Association, put it succinctly: Cable TV has become the MIRVs of politics. The messages are independently targeted reentry vehicles. A politician can send a different message to every audience, as Barney Frank's were targeted both geographically and demographically. A candidate using cable *knows* that whoever *is* watching is someone who can vote for him. The candidate is getting more bang for his bucks.[7]

The future portends many more cable campaigns. Not only is it politically astute, but also far less expensive than the conventional mass media campaign. Cable is the ideal bedfellow of coalition politics.

Demassification—it is a prerequisite for cable TV stage two: direct democracy utilizing an interactive system. Seen in its most favorable light, cable TV and its companion technology are in the highest ideals of the humanistic tradition.[8] One author contemplating the impact of cable sees it leading to greater "political participation and justice for the 'know-nots' and 'have-nots.' "[9]

That is truly a worthy end of politics. Direct participation is a positive good, as long as the fabric of the American system remains intact. But what is the route? How can the long dormant philosophy of Rousseau be harnessed to the developing technology? How can the nation retain the virtues of representative government and still value direct participation?

Traveling the highway to tomorrow requires a glance at the past. As the British political commentator Edmund Burke once said, political society is a contract between the dead, the living, and the unborn.

Perhaps no foreign-born political thinker influenced the formative stage of American government more than John Locke. Locke studied ancient Athens and concluded that a face-to-face assembly was not needed to make democracy work. Rather, the representatives only needed a sense of obligation to the people who elected them.[10] By nature, stated Locke, man was pleasure-seeking, even selfish, some would argue. That did not mean that a monarchy or aristocracy was needed to hold self-interest in check.

Locke contended that man was, above all, reasonable. And Locke had faith in reason. He had so much faith that he believed reason could unify a society composed of many groups pursuing selfish economic interests. Locke had little faith that people pursuing personal goals would care much about the other person. But under his political philosophy, harmony of interest was unnecessary.

The rational person would listen to the discussion of various viewpoints, formulate his own opinion, and retain a general belief that the majority is correct.[11] A contemporary might refer to the eighteenth-century concept as pooled intelligence. Rational people acting together make rational decisions.

Factions of private interest were worrisome. But they could be harnessed. The Hobbesian would favor a strong monarchy to counteract factions, while the follower of Locke would welcome factions because reason always prevails. As the conservative believes dire consequences result from the dispersal of power, the disciple of Locke argues that the dispersal of power is an essential ingredient of social order.

It was out of this school of political philosophy that the Founding Fathers came. For obvious reasons they rejected monarchy. The only aristocracy that appealed to them was an aristocracy of merit and that seemed impractical. But *factions*—organized groups trying to influence society—could be the glue holding the great democratic experiment together. Modern political scientists would call these theorists pluralists.

In the world of the pluralist, struggle is resolved through negotiation, bargaining, and compromise.[12] The only rule is that all factions accept the outcome of the compromises. In the pluralist system no combination of groups can form a permanent majority. If competing pressure groups do not control decision making, democracy falls victim to either the tyranny of the majority or the selfish rule of an aristocracy.

Federalist author James Madison saw it clearly: ambition must be employed to counteract ambition; the passion of one must be used to balance the passion of another. Politics based on the competition of interest groups is aimed at *avoiding* class struggle, which, Madison knew, had previously been the downfall of popular governments.[13]

As the Founding Fathers anticipated, America was to become a society of diversity, of unleashed commercialism and acquisitiveness. At the same time, American society would be a champion of "durable decency," where public affairs would be conducted in an atmosphere of "public spiritedness."[14]

The essence of pluralism is that everyone gets what he needs as long as he is organized. That has been the golden rule of American politics. To the organized go the spoils of society. Under the pluralistic model, the individual is seen as a political consumer. The more the individual puts in, the more he gets out.[15] Pluralism rejects as simplistic the arguments of both the liberals and conservatives. To the pluralist, whether or not the individual embodies goodness and virtue is irrelevant. It is also unimportant whether or not an aristocracy is essential for political stability. Stability is to be found in the balancing of interests. Insight into human nature won't make the system work, says the pluralist. The philosophy is pure pragmatism. Those who are more ambitious and invest more time and energy into the system will get more out of it. When the ship of state is driven by the tug of competing ambition, its course should be dead center. So it has been with only slight deviation through all of American history.

Perhaps it would be best to think of the authors of the Constitution as qualified democrats. True mass participation was not relevant to their experience. In Massachusetts, for example, a man had to belong to the Congregational Church before being enfranchised. In Pennsylvania the vote was restricted to those who owned property valued in excess of fifty pounds. In Virginia a voter had to possess fifty acres of land or a house and twenty-five acres. In South Carolina voters had to be members of the Church of England. In general, the vote in Colonial times was given to white male property holders who paid taxes and belonged to a particular religious denomination.[16]

Moreover, many of the nation's founders had strong antidemocratic biases:

> The majority of the signers of the Declaration of Independence had not taken that fateful step in order to deliver themselves into the hands of the "back-country levellers" or "town mobs." . . .Their principle aim was to take over the power that had been exercised by British officials, without changing the existing class and political structure in other ways.[17]

At the Constitutional Convention William Livingston of New Jersey was quoted as saying, "The people ever have been and ever will be unfit to retain the exercise of power in their own hands." Alexander Hamilton of New York spoke of the "imprudence of democracy." His thoughts were echoed by Edmund Randolph of Virginia, who blamed the chaos and economic dislocation after the Revolution to "the turbulence and follies of democracy." Charles Pinckney of South Carolina suggested high property qualifications for federal office holders.[18]

These powerful antidemocratic feelings resulted in a Constitution in which powers were separated and each branch of government was restricted through an elaborate, though brilliant, system of checks and balances. The legislature was divided into two houses; the president could veto and the legislature could by a clear majority override the chief executive. The Constitution itself could only be changed by two-thirds of both houses and then ratified by three-quarters of the state legislatures. The system went on and on—lifetime appointments for the judiciary to insulate them from political passions. An election every second year for members of the House of Representatives to expose them to those same political passions. The president was checked by the Senate on treaties and appointments; the House of Representatives had the honor of initiating revenue legislation.The president would be chosen by electors and the senators by state legislators. The final consensus in Philadelphia produced a government both restrained and prudent. The idea was to place the various branches of government in a perpetual tug-of-war in which none of the sides would ever have a significant advantage.

Hamilton clearly expressed the general sentiments of the Founding Fathers regarding the people's ability to rule: "All communities divide themselves into the few and the many. The first are the rich and well-born: the other, the mass of people who seldom judge or determine right."[19] For Hamilton, and to a large extent Jefferson, the new government was to be one ruled by talented men of wealth and leisure.

The Founding Fathers, those democrats of convenience, put together a remarkable system. It did achieve its stated goal—to avoid the historic conflicts of popular rule. Factions were intentionally set in conflict and the result is two centuries of political consistency.

Despite all the safeguards against genuine popular rule, the seeds Rousseau planted continued to germinate. But it would take two centuries of technological advancement before Rousseau's ideas could become practical.

It has long been assumed that direct democracy is inherently incompatible with the pluralistic model. The American system of dispersed federal power among executive, legislative, and judicial branches serves to contain the potential dangers of pluralism. There are thousands of lobbyists prowling Capitol Hill; more than a thousand Political Action Committees (PAC) contribute to Congressional campaigns; the force of public opinion also plays heavily on the legislative branch. The same can be said for the executive branch. Interest groups representing many thousands of constituencies continually seek to influence policy in the executive branch. And the federal judiciary remains an avenue of redress for groups contending that their legal rights have been violated.

The states have a mirror system of government. In addition, the multitude of local governments within each state also aid in controlling the possible excesses of factions.

The Madisonian system has allowed the nation to survive when many governments in sister democracies have stumbled. No majority has held the public stage for long: not business, not labor; not the military, not the intellectuals; not the WASPs, not the ethnics; not the cities, not the farms; not the rich, not the poor. Each faction, at one time or another, has had its moment of glory and moment of defeat. It would be folly to tamper dramatically with the existing American system.

Along comes a technology which cannot be denied. Whether it is fulfilling the promise of corporate America today is unimportant—at some point the technology of interactive cable will be in place. How could any rational person ever believe that a technology which is in the home and does the family shopping, entertaining, and educating will not be employed in the political process?

Thus the new technology necessarily challenges the pluralist model. It writes in bold strokes—citizen, you do not have to belong to a particular special interest group to participate. Whether you're a member of the National Rifle Association or Handgun Control is unimportant. You, citizen, have power.

The cornerstone of pluralist theory is *citizen apathy*.[20] As the theory goes, the common good emerges from the clash of special interests. Public opinion is of secondary importance because (until now) it was hard to measure. The public has been quick to follow interest groups and politicians.[21] The public rarely leads.

In the world of the pluralist one has to join an interest group to be an effective player. Otherwise, one is consigned to vote only on election day and otherwise sit on the sidelines during the debate over policy.

Political theorist Edmund Burke saw democracy as power *delegated* from voter to representative. Once elected, Burke argued, representatives ignore constituents and concentrate on conscience.[22] American legislators have historically been torn between Burke's admonition against following the dictates of a constituency and the political realism of seeing oneself as an agent of the constituency. Polls indicate that Americans think of their legislators as agents, not independent delegates.[23]

Thus it appears that people want to be more involved. Apathy does not have to be a political fact of life. Clearly, statistics of voter turnout do not support increased participation. Yet it must be argued that the desire to vote in a primary or general election is far different from the desire to participate in the formation of policy. If given the opportunity, many more people might exercise their franchise if they were voting on *issues* rather than a stranger's tenure in office.

What strikes directly at the pluralist model is the rising phenomenon of *issue* groups. There is an enormous difference between *issue* groups and *interest* groups—the latter is the pillar of pluralist government and the former is the companion of direct democracy. Issue groups have been loosely categorized under the heading of single issue politics. Basically formed along *ethical* principles, with loyalty based upon *ethics*, economic self-interest is not relevant to the individual aligned with an issue group.[24] Typical issue group concerns are abortion, disarmament, homosexual rights, guns, feminism, tax reform, and the environment. Often the issue groups are so broadly defined that almost anyone agreeing with the group's ethical principles can find a home. For example, the Moral Majority and Common Cause are issue groups appealing to millions of individuals without regard to economic factors. Contemplating the rise of issue groups, *Newsweek* observed that, "From grass roots to Capitol Hill the nation is caught up in a rugged new game of single issue politics. Every conceivable issue seems to have competing pressure groups." [25]

Issue groups implicitly advance participatory democracy because they claim to speak for the majority.

In sharp contrast, the traditional *interest* groups—the bricks of Madisonian pluralism—claim to speak for a specific economic point of view on social policy. The National Association of Manufacturers speaks for business. The American Federation of Labor speaks for labor. The NAACP speaks for black Americans. The VFW speaks for veterans. With these and thousands of other groups, there is no pretense of speaking for everyone. Having a narrow constituency, the interest group is well suited to dealing in the pluralist arena. Bargaining and compromise are givens. To lose means to come back and fight another day. To win means to respect the loser because he may eventually gain the upper hand. Consensus on those rules is what made the representative system function and kept factions in check. John Locke understood that.

But issue groups, committed to ethical principles, leave virtually no room to maneuver or bargain. In addition, with whom does an issue group check to see if compromise is acceptable? If the group contends that is speaks for a *majority*, why should there be debate, compromise, and bargaining at all?

The brilliantly crafted American system was not structured to cope with the ascendance of issue groups. The basic assumption that man forms political factions to advance economic self-interest is less credible when people forsake economic gains for ethical goals. The issue groups philosophically and practically are in no position to bargain and compromise with the legislative and executive branches of government. In a phrase, they don't want to play by the rules.

The rhetoric of issue groups hearkens back to the dreamers of a pure democracy. These groups appeal to the majority, to a sense of right and wrong. Coalition politics is alien. To these groups the traditional give and take of the Madisonian process taints and blemishes their cause. Democracy, for them, has greater appeal than politics as usual, the rough and tumble of compromise or coalition-building.

The ever-growing phenomenon of issue groups is symptomatic of pressure from within the body politic for greater direct participation. The issues have always existed. But in recent years people have begun to realize that pluralist politics can balance competing economic interests better than it can resolve nagging ethical questions. It should come as no revelation that in an age of comparative affluence, it is easier for people to pursue ethical issues—issues unrelated to economic survival—than in hard economic times.

The public mood demands some alternative to the pluralist system. An outlet must be provided for public participation in a forum other than the existing representative system. Perhaps without realizing it, the issue groups are asking for a return to the philosophic roots of the system. Jean Jacques Rousseau would applaud their efforts. For nothing is lost and everything gained, he would say, when power resides with the majority.

Today, with the technology capable of effecting a direct democracy, the call of the new issue groups takes on a greater urgency. While it would be ill-advised to tamper with the foundations of the American political system, the time when democratic experimentation is appropriate is at hand. The system is resilient. Change is not an enemy of democracy. Larry the Lobster doesn't have to be only a joke.

Notes

1.   Keith Michael Baker, "To Be Free and Still Belong," *New York Times Book Review* (September 16, 1984): 9.

2.   Leslie Lipson, *The Democratic Civilization* (New York: Oxford Univ. Press, 1964, 43.

3.   Baker, "To Be Free and Still Belong," 9.

4.   Austin Ranney and Willmore Kendall, *Democracy and the American Party System* (New York: Harcourt, Brace & Co., 1956), 41.

5.   Alvin Toffler, *The Third Wave* (New York: William Morrow & Co., 1980), 424.

6.   Richard Armstrong, "Gutter Politics in the Global Village," *National Review*, 36, no. 7 (April 20, 1984): 30.

7.   Ibid., 32.

8.   Martin Diamond, in Irving Kristol and Paul H. Weaver, eds., *The Americans 1976* (Lexington, Mass.: Lexington Books, 1976), 13.

9.   Neil Hurley, "The Wired Home, An Information Utility," *America*, 139, no. 18, December 2, 1978, 104.

10. Ranney and Kendall, *Democracy*, 9.

11. C. Wright Mills, *Power, Politics and People* (New York: Oxford Univ. Press, 1963), 580.

12. Livingston and Thompson, *Consent of the Governed*, 85.

13. Ranney and Kendall, *Democracy*, 41.

14. Diamond, *The Americans*, 14 and 19.

15. Livingston and Thompson, *Consent of the Governed*, 123.

16. Harry J. Carman, Harold C. Syrett, and Bernard W. Wishy, *A History of the American People*, vol. 2 (New York: Alfred A. Knopf, 1961), 129.

17. Ibid., 231.

18. Ibid., 252.

19. Ibid.

20. Sylvia Tesh, "In Support of 'Single Issue' Politics," *Political Science Quarterly* 99, no. 1 (Spring 1984): 43.

21. Robert Shapiro and Benjamin Page, "Effects of Public Opinion on Police," *American Political Science Review* 77, no. 1 (March 1983): 181.

22. Ranney and Kendall, *Democracy*, 72.

23. Ibid., 76.

24. Tesh, "In Support," 28.

25. Ibid., *Newsweek*, November 6, 1978, cited in Tesh, ibid., 31.

4

THE EXTENSION
OF DEMOCRACY

FORGET THE FOUNDING Fathers and their trust in the pluralist system. Direct democracy has won few converts in the succeeding two-hundred years. As a system of government, direct democracy has been about as popular as the plague in seventeenth-century London.

There are several reasons why those who think about and practice politics have distanced themselves from direct democracy. First, it was always seen as highly impractical. Why write about a theory if the only place it can be seen to work is a New England town meeting or a high school senior class? Secondly, it would quite naturally never occur to the practitioners of government, the politicians, that public life could exist without them. Elected leaders are not very likely to suggest that there is an alternative way of running government. Finally, the people who write about such things—the scholars, politicians, and journalists—have a generally intellectual orientation, which precludes their conceiving of the masses doing a reasonable job of running government on a day-to-day basis. So, direct democracy has long been relegated to the backwater of political theory. When the subject has come up, the response has largely been negative, if not hostile, an idea scorned by scholars: "The image of a society in which all men are wholly devoted to the great public business is worse than utopian. It is disagreeable." [1]

Intellectuals compare democracy to a ship; the passengers must never take over its actual navigation. The proper role for passengers is to select the destination and leave the navigation to experienced seamen. Dr. Milton Eisenhower, the former president of The Johns Hopkins University in Baltimore, had been an advisor to eight presidents and an actor on the world stage for six decades. His view of direct democracy in any form was that it is outright dangerous: "Not one in 100; not one in 1,000 understands the causes of inflation, the balance of trade or any other major world issue," said Eisenhower emphatically. "I'm exceedingly skeptical on mass judgment. The people are not informed. Mass judgment is simply no good."[2]

Dr. Joseph Foley of the Communications Department at Ohio State University in Columbus has studied QUBE and contemplated what its advent means to democracy. He believes the company behind QUBE, Warner-Amex, has not devoted much computer or brain time to the issue. "For them [QUBE] it's more like 'now that we have the buttons what are we going to do to make them [the viewers] happy they have the buttons'," Foley explained. The communications professor went on to say that he is certain QUBE viewers are not representative of anything except the kind of person who would watch TV test patterns if "General Hospital" were not on. "It's the TV junkie who is likely to push buttons. The person sitting there pushing buttons may not be the guy going to public hearings. It is likely to be the guy who likes game shows and sees the town meeting on QUBE as just another quiz show."[3]

The operative theory in America has been that since people are not angels, direct democracy cannot work. Leave government to the smart; if not the smart, then the powerful. Yet very slowly, almost without notice and certainly without acclaim, discussion about direct democracy has begun to creep into the public discourse. In 1965, V. K. Zworykin wrote that the world in 1984 would see national questions broadcast over TV and radio. Telephone responses, he predicted, "would bring about close alignment of policy and opinion." Nineteen eighty-four did not bring direct democracy in any form. Nevertheless, the level of interest in true popular rule *has* been elevated. Alvin Toffler, in *Future Shock*, envisioned "a continuing plebiscite on the future . . . [which would] turn out to be the salvation of representative politics—a system now in dire crisis."[4]

Much of the growing interest in direct democracy can be traced to QUBE and similar interactive systems. In the spring of 1981, members of Congress had the opportunity to have an electronic dialogue with QUBE subscribers in Columbus. Organized by the House Telecommunications Subcommittee, the system used a two-way satellite hookup between Capitol Hill and Columbus. Congressmen were able to pose questions to the good citizens of Columbus and receive responses in percentage form. Subcommittee chairman Timothy Wirth, D-Col., called interactive TV a very promising means of gauging public opinion. Rep. Michael Barnes, D-Md., was outright gleeful. "I'm very envious of the people of Columbus. I wish we had this in my home state of Maryland."[5]

In recent years, some have tried to make direct democracy work. Make it practical. Adopt the hardware to the theory and field test the system. Sometimes in history theory precedes practice and sometimes it is the reverse.

To this end, Amitai Etzioni and Associates developed a system called MINERVA, named after the Roman goddess of wisdom. MINERVA attempts to convene a gigantic town meeting providing for dialogue and instant feedback. Small groups of thirty are linked via telephone into a discussion group. These groups are then hooked up with the larger community over two-way cable TV. Issues are first discussed in the small groups, then among the community at large. Theoretically, 10,000 people can participate in the MINERVA system. A reasonable logistical problem arises. What if two hundred people want to talk at the same time? That is resolved by approval and disapproval buttons on each keypad. If a citizen doesn't like what a speaker is saying, just give him the hook with an electronic vote of no confidence.[6]

Perhaps the most far-reaching experiment in direct democracy has been carried out by a computer firm call Applied Futures, Inc. The high-tech company, headed by former IBM executive William Simmons, has taken a device named CONSENSOR into the world of politics and concluded that direct democracy is technically feasible. The origins of CONSENSOR have nothing to do with politics. It was invented to fill a need Simmons believed existed in corporate boardrooms. The aim of CONSENSOR, said Simmons, was "to find out how much they [the members of a board of directors] know and how strongly they feel about alternative choices facing them."[7] As Simmons saw it, there were three problems at corporate meetings: a lack of participation, a fear of exposing one's views too openly, and an inability to quantify opinions. To rectify those problems Simmons came up with CONSENSOR, the R2-D2 of direct democracy.

CONSENSOR is nothing more than a little box with two dials—one dial for voting and the other dial for "weighting" the vote. The voting dial is marked zero through ten and the weighting dial is marked in increments of twenty-five up to one hundred. The weighting dial records percentages of the vote—or *intensity* of feeling. The magic of CONSENSOR is that it factors together both priority and intensity. By contrast, QUBE and other two-way cable systems only measure priority. Aside from the CONSENSOR gadgetry, the system needs a TV screen and a control console. With the hardware in place, it is possible to measure support or opposition to an issue and expertise or confidence one has in his own opinion. If the readout on the terminal shows the bars on the graph clustered together, then one has a consensus among those seated around the boardroom table. According to Simmons, "The CONSENSOR offers a way to make business meetings and public discussions shorter, more productive, and, at the same time, more democratic and more representative of the participants' true feelings."

Simmons has used CONSENSOR for such everyday decisions as selecting a destination for a vacation. Simmons and a group of friends wanted to vacation together, but, like any group, could not agree on where to go. Better than counting hands, CONSENSOR would mathematically weigh and compare the votes of those who mildly favored the Caribbean beach over the Rocky Mountain ski trip with those who passionately wanted the ski trip and were strongly opposed to the island vacation. Carried to an extreme, CONSENSOR could eliminate many family squabbles because it gives extra weight to the votes of those who have intense feelings on particular issues. It takes a giant step beyond the age-old concept of majority rule.

But CONSENSOR is far more than a new parlor game. It might be as much fun as Space Invaders, but its implication for the practice of politics is staggering. CONSENSOR, assisted by broadcast journalist Daniel Schorr, was taken to Alaska where it presided over statewide town meetings—direct democracy come alive. Alaska has the delicious dilemma of disposing an annual budget surplus. State law requires legislators to attend town meetings around the state before voting on the allocation of the budget surplus. Over a period of nine nights in the fall of 1979, town meetings were held in Anchorage, Fairbanks, Sitka, Juneau, Kenai, and Ketchikan. At each meeting, ninety participants who were statistically representative of the population were given CONSENSOR voting terminals. Citizens at home could watch the televised town meetings and vote by telephone. Moderator Schorr, located in the KIMO-TV studios in Anchorage, gave background on such issues as mass transit, road improvements, ferry service, jails, exploration for natural gas, and port improvements. Following Schorr's discourse, citizens holding the terminals responded by turning the dials on CONSENSOR left or right—yes or no—to increase or decrease funding of a particular project. Then they voted on how strongly they felt by turning the intensity dial. In all, Alaskans were asked twenty-two questions and the results of each were tabulated and displayed on the home TV screen within one minute. After the various votes, Schorr held a question and answer session with state legislators and local officials. In retrospect, Schorr called the votes meaningful, especially when the CONSENSOR voters were presented with trade-offs. For example, initially the participants were supportive of road improvements, but they backed off from their endorsement when told of the inevitable rise in carbon monoxide pollution. Many hailed CONSENSOR's Alaskan debut for providing "full, anonymous and instantaneous quantified feedback from the citizenry."

CONSENSOR did not win over the hearts of all Alaskans. One newspaper dubbed it "an Orwellian little device." Michael Porcaro, executive director of the Alaska Public Broadcasting Commission, condemned the experiment, saying the end product was "homogeneous mediocrity." Bob Arnold, former director of Alaska's broadcasting commission, charged that "Any official who fights the CONSENSOR is opening himself up to charges that he is bucking the public will. We can handicap the political leadership by showing a consensus that is based on ill-formed opinions." CONSENSOR can, of course, factor in or give less weight to those opinions which are ill-informed. That is contingent only on the honesty of the voter. If he believes his vote is uninformed, he should say so when using the intensity dial.

To Schorr's final question, Do you favor televised town meetings, 94 percent answered affirmatively.

Why electronic democracy? The most obvious answer is that the extension of the franchise across the cable is nothing more than the continuation of a two-hundred-year-old process. Democracy in the United States has never been static. The pool of those eligible to vote has grown ever larger from the earliest days of the Republic until today. One can argue against the advent of direct democracy on the grounds that it might change the chemistry of a very delicate political system. And there is merit to that position. But it cannot be argued that direct democracy runs counter to history. Franchise extension is a fundamental thread in the American political fabric. A brief look at this trend indicates that it is wholly consistent with the past and totally just.

Universal suffrage in the United States was very slow in coming. The authors of the Constitution were not especially interested in bringing people to the polls. For example, James Madison, no hero to romantic democrats, had a strong aversion to universal suffrage. Madison saw a future industrial world with a large proletariat underclass. At the Constitutional Convention, Madison wrote, "In England, at this day, if the elections were open to all classes of people, the property of the landed proprietors would be insecure."[8] John Adams, the second president, was equally distressed over the prospect of awarding the vote indiscriminately. In a letter on the extension of suffrage, Adams said,

> It would be dangerous to open so fruitful a source of controversy and altercation as would be opened by attempting to alter the qualifications of voters; there will be no end to it. New claims will arise; women will demand a vote; lads from 12 to 21 will think their rights not enough attended to; and every man who has not a farthing will demand an equal voice with any other. . . .[9]

Adams was not speaking solely in abstract terms. His wife, Abigail, who was said to be at least equal to her husband in intelligence and wit, saw no reason why her sex should be denied the vote. Why, Mrs. Adams asked, should women be bound by laws when "we have no voice in representation"?[10] Adams thought his wife was joking. She wasn't.

The great bogeyman of the mob rule prevailed in Philadelphia and the men who wrote the Constitution must have gone home convinced they had saved the young Republic from the propertyless and godless rabble. But in the new Constitution and particularly in the first ten amendments, the seeds were sown for universal manhood and womanhood suffrage. It would be a battle which would extend well into the contemporary era and beyond. Its enemies would be fear, ignorance, and prejudice. Even in the late eighteenth century, the outcome of the struggle was clear. The very spirit of America could not deny the vote to a citizen. As Thomas Paine said of the right to vote, some nineteen years after the signing of the Declaration, "To take away this right [the vote] is to reduce a man to a state of slavery, for slavery consists in being a subject to the will of another."[11] The right of assembly, the right to petition the government, the guarantee of a free press, and the philosophic commitment to majority rule all paved the way for the painstaking expansion of suffrage.

Over the course of American history there were periods of backsliding, to be sure. Blacks continued to vote for a generation after reconstruction. But such savage barriers as the literacy test, the poll tax, and the grandfather clause successfully disenfranchised Southern blacks long after the fifteenth Amendment supposedly awarded the vote to the former slaves. So complete was the political emasculation of blacks that as recently as 1965, only 26,000 of Mississippi's nearly half million blacks could vote.

Without reviewing in detail the tragic, often brutal history of the blacks' quest for the vote, it should be affirmed again that the issue was never more complex than a group demanding simple justice. As the Catholic journal *America* stated so clearly in June 1963, "patience is not an end in itself." By the mid-1960s time had run out on the bigots, the states' righters, and the politically timid. A few months later, one *America* editorial writer said, "The work of Lincoln will finally be done only when the American Negro at last is fully freed from the bondage of slavery."[12]

The conscience of America had been stirred. What was abandoned as hopeless had been brought to life in a matter of a few short years. Television dramatized the full horror of civil rights denied. The cattle prods, dogs, fire hoses, and abuse heaped upon those who asked nothing more than full citizenship including the right to vote was caught by the television. Also trapped in the lens of the news photographer was the religious dignity of nonviolent demonstrators.

It was the day of the famous Selma march. There were a thousand demonstrators and two-hundred police. Many of Selma's whites watched the events on TV, much like the rest of the nation.

"Turn off that set," a white man in the saloon yelled, sipping a beer with a crowd of other whites today in Selma.
"Yeah, I'm getting tired of seeing niggers on TV."
"You're tired," another man said, "but those niggers ain't."[13]

By the 1960s, television had become a means of extending the vote. Even without television, the cause of black voting rights would have triumphed. TV did speed up the political process, but at some point a president would have said what Lyndon Johnson did before a joint session of Congress on March 15, 1965: "about this there can and should be no argument; every American citizen must have an equal right to vote. . . . It is wrong—deadly wrong—to deny any of your fellow Americans the right to vote in this country."[14] Johnson noted in his text that "the real heart of the battle is a deep-seated belief in the democratic process."[15] It was the legacy from the Declaration of Independence and the spirit of the revolution—someday the franchise must be given freely to all.

Blacks were not the only group left outside the polling place. It was not until the mid-nineteenth-century that most states abolished property qualifications for voting. The election of 1840 is seen by historians as the first national election of universal white male suffrage. In that year Martin VanBuren ran against William Henry Harrison for president.

Two and one half million votes were cast, double that of the presidential election of 1832. Property barriers were falling, but Jews, Indians, Chinese, and any other group perceived as undesirable could not vote until roughly the turn of the century.

Women—though totaling half the population—were excluded from the political picture through most of American history. By the turn of the century, only Wyoming, Colorado, Utah, and Idaho had given women full voting rights. Then the movement snowballed. There were petitions, demonstrations, parades, pamphleting, and picketing. In June 1919, with the support of the Wilson administration, Congress approved the Constitutional amendment giving women the right to vote. It was ratified fourteen months later.

The 1920 election, the first in which women could vote, saw a 45 percent increase in the number of votes cast. During the campaign, no one—including the candidates—knew whether the newly enfranchised women would vote for Democrat James Cox or Republican Warren Harding. A few weeks before election day, candidate Harding, speaking from the rear platform of his campaign train in Scottsburg, Indiana, said: "It was my good fortune to have voted for the suffrage amendment and I do not ever want to regret it. The only thing in the world that could make me regret voting for women's suffrage would be for the women to undertake to have a party of their own."[16]

With historic hindsight, it seems almost absurd that Harding would even speculate about a woman's party. Harding's statement merely serves to indicate that in 1920 few really understood the political impact of suffrage. What Harding did understand was that women's voting rights were part of America forever. He knew that male politicians would be incapable of altering the momentum of history.

In the United States, that momentum means a continual expansion of the electoral base. Indeed, there have been exceptions, the most notable being the disenfranchisement of Southern blacks in the post Reconstruction era. Nevertheless, even the most cursory glance at American policital history supports the theory of expanding the number of voters. Is it not possible that the same historical forces are at work today? Why not equate the coming of video democracy with the extension of the vote to women and all the suffrage movements which came before?

Critics contend that at-home voting disrupts the slow, dispassionate, reasoned process of indirect democracy. They worry about the effects of video democracy on the quality of leadership. They argue that the system works only when people vote for candidates and not issues.

Are these criticisms echos of Harding? Are they just as unfounded as Harding's concerns about the newly enfranchised women forming their own political party? Someday people may find it absurd that some theorists in the mid-1980s raised such questions about direct democracy. Ridiculous arguments abound when we look back at the periods when the vote was given to the propertyless, the non-Christians, blacks, and women. History alone must judge whether any effort to expand democracy is reasonable. So far, history has no regrets.

Examine the extension of the vote to 18-year-olds, for example. In 1970, a Gallup poll showed student unrest to be the number one American problem, overshadowing Vietnam, inflation, and race relations. At the same time, TV viewers saw young Americans bleeding in the rice paddies. It seemed fair—though there was opposition—that the vote had to be given to the young as a gesture offering them a stake in the system.

Whether one is talking about the poor, women, blacks, or the young; whether the year is 1840, 1919, 1965, or 1970, the message is clear. The historic mandate appears to have a momentum of its own. America constantly expands its electorate.

Today, with every ethnic, gender, economic, and age group enfranchised, what is the next frontier? It is to be found in the revolution of interactive television. The day is not far when it *will* be argued that allowing a person to vote through his television is quite essential to the civil rights of the elderly, the infirm, the handicapped, and others who find it a hardship to go to the polls. There is much merit to that argument. We live in a time when the rights of the aged are being addressed in Congress and in legislative bodies across the nation. The same is true for the handicapped. Having a polling place around the corner, down the block, or a mile away limits participation of the old and disabled much as the poll tax kept many Southern blacks away from the ballot box. The supporters of such a plan will say that an absentee ballot does not compensate for a lack of physical proximity. Feebleness in body should not bring with it a loss of civil rights. Now the technology exists to bring the polling place to the voter. Besides, putting the vote in the voter's home is less expensive than buying voting machines and hiring all sorts of poll judges and administrators.

The slow but inexorable process of broadening the American electoral base should include the video vote, which is not to be confused with video democracy. The video vote merely means moving the ballot box from the polling place to the TV set. If applied universally, the video vote would enormously increase voter participation. Regardless of whether true video democracy is practiced, this country would be well served by experimentation with at-home voting. The technology, demand, and historic precedent exist for such a trial. Video voting itself does not necessarily advance video democracy.

Assuming that at-home voting increases participation, video voting can be justified as a means of exorcising the demon of citizen apathy. No democracy, representative or direct, can long function if election day is seen as little more than a day to take advantage of shopping mall sales. The survival of the system rests on the awareness that a critical mass must participate in elections if people are to follow government policy. An extreme lesson of nonparticipation occurred in 1928, when more than 25 percent of the German electorate refused to vote in the Reichstag election. That poorly conceived protest greatly increased Hitler's chances.[17]

In the present era, turnouts in presidential elections hover around 50 percent of eligible voters, and in Congressional races the turnout can be as low as 35 percent. In local elections, campaigns can be won by well-organized minorities. In the 1880s and 1890s more than 75 percent of the voting age population regularly cast ballots on election day. Contemporary America has witnessed the triumph of apathy over participation. The pluralist system of representative government devised by the Founding Fathers can well withstand the assaults of conflict, but it may be endangered by those who choose to ignore the ballot box. "Voters voluntarily avoid the booth because they see no connection between politics and their lives," said Arthur Hadley in *The Empty Polling Booth.* "The crucial fact—never spoken, ever present truth—is that Americans have given up their citizenship."[18]

Rather than lamenting the disintegration of citizenship values, we could easily reinvigorate the system by allowing people to vote at home. When that event occurs—and it appears to be historic inevitability—nothing will have changed the representative system. People will still vote for candidates, not policies. The technology for direct democracy will be in the front door, with the blessing of government, no less.

What about this system called democracy? Why have Americans been driven by an internal force always to expand the system? Why care if the poor have the vote, or blacks, or women or the young? What value is there in this method of government borrowed from Periclean Athens?

"Vox populi, vox dei"—the voice of the people is the voice of God. It is the democratic creed. Americans believe it not only because it was the handed-down wisdom of junior high civics texts, but also because it makes sense. A case can be made for democracy without resorting to romantic sentiment. The world is neither too technical nor too complex for democracy to be buried in the graveyard of obsolete political systems. Whether applied in the representative model or a direct democracy, mass popular participation is an eminently logical and reasonable system of government. It has been much maligned, but never willingly discarded. There is nothing mysterious or difficult about democcracy. Democracy is comfortable, like an old pair of loafers. It gives societies a great sense of reassurance.[19] It provides the most peaceful method of all in determining who shall hold power. Democracy creates stability in its very instability. Power changes hands so swiftly in a democracy. Elections are frequent; the ins are out and the outs are in. Like ballast on a ship, the very frequency of elections serves to keep society on an even keel.

Far from the perfect and predictable fit of hand in glove, no guarantee of personal liberty exists de facto in a democracy. Liberty may exist under a monarchy or an oligarchy or any number of systems. And there can be democracy without personal liberty but not without political liberty. That is the necessary qualifier. Once there are competitive elections, then the opposition must have liberties and protections. Companion institutions—the courts, the press, and political parties—are the natural offspring of political liberty. It would be most difficult to structure a democratic society without insuring a high degree of political liberty.

Another characteristic of democracy is that it provides for a social consensus.[20] People believe it is *their* government, and that, in turn, forms bonds between the ruler and the ruled. To voice displeasure with public policy is not an act of disloyalty, but an act of independence. One can feel at home in the system even though he disagrees with governmental policy. The arms of democracy embrace the dissenters as well as those who support the existing power structure. Social consensus is achieved by respect for the opinions of the minority.

As mentioned, conflict does not threaten democracy. Individuals and groups are expected to win with humility and lose with honor. Each election, each vote is no more important than the one before or the one yet to come. The very nature of democracy blunts conflicts and turns competition into a unifying force.

Finally, democracy survives because power is not isolated. The process of government demands interaction between the rulers and the ruled.[21] When people are asked their opinions, bridges are built and, by definition, power is shared.

It is thus no accident of history that American democracy has produced a remarkably stable and politically effective government. The democratic attitude is responsible for the vitality of the system.[22] American democracy is forever new and forever alive, vibrant with ideas and innovation. "At bottom the democratic attitude is simply an attitude of good faith plus a working belief in the probable rationality of others."[23] The eleventh commandment of democracy is that people hold no irreversible opinions. Change is part of the natural order because every ear is listening and every mind is open. Closed minds invite a closed society.

Democracy is like a well-designed bridge. It is balanced, stable, flexible, adjusts to change, and carries the heaviest traffic under the worst conditions.

Democracy is no more than the sum of its parts. The strength of the system is conditional on faith in the common man. A society can be both democratic and free only when the people rule in fact as well as in theory. "In the long run, the common man collectively is a better judge as to what is good for him than any self-appointed elite."[24]

There is no true democracy without universal acceptance of the moral and intellectual character of the average person. Elites assert their leadership on the assumption that the future is uncertain and only the experts, those endowed with extraordinary qualities, can lead. The reality is that no one can ever know if the leadership of the elite is right or wrong. In the absense of proof, democratic theory says, "trust the people." This reverence for the common man can be outlined in three propositions:

—Ordinary men will attempt to get all the facts.
—Ordinary men will reach sensible conclusions.
—Ordinary men will act rationally.[25]

Democracy does not need special justifications. One can accept democracy without qualification.

American political life has been through many changes since its inception. Its health is a tribute to institutions which adapt to a fluid political environment. More importantly, perhaps, Americans have heeded in spirit, if not always in practice, "vox populi, vox dei."

Notes

1.   Charles Frankel, *The Democratic Prospect* (New York: Harper and Row, 1962), 45.

2.   Milton Eisenhower, former president, The Johns Hopkins University, Baltimore, Md., personal interview, May 21, 1981.

3.   Joseph Foley, Communications Department, Ohio State University, Columbus, Ohio, personal interview, August 26, 1981.

4.   Alvin Toffler, *Future Shock* (New York: Bantam Books, originally published by Random House, 1971), 477-83.

5.   "Spring Brings New Technology Exhibition to Capitol Hill," *Broadcasting* 100, no. 13 (March 30, 1981): 53.

6.   Robert Weissberg, *Public Opinion and Popular Government* (Englewood Cliffs, N.J.: Prentice-Hall, 1976), 75.

7.   William W. Simmons, president, Applied Futures, Inc., Greenwich, Conn., corporate correspondence, 1978-1980. All Simmons quotes are taken from this material.

8.   Marchette Chute, *The First Liberty* (New York: E. P. Dutton & Co., 1969), 251.

9.   Ibid., 196.

10.   Ibid., 315.

11.   Ibid., 195.

12.   "Abraham Lincoln Unfinished Business," (editorial) *America* 110, no. 6 (February 8, 1964): 183.

13.   Gay Talese, "Selma: Bitter City in the Eye of a Storm,"*New York Times*, March 14, 1965.

14.   Lyndon Johnson, "The Right to Vote," *Vital Speeches* 31, no. 12 (April 1, 1965): 354-57.

15.   Ibid., 356.

16.   Warren Harding, quoted in the *New York Times*, October 16, 1920.

17.   "Electoral Values Old and New," *Saturday Review* 54, no. 22 (May 29, 1971): 16.

18.   Arthur Hadley, in Kirkpatrick Sale, "Why Voters Don't Care," *The Nation* 230, no. 21 (May 31, 1980); : 654.

19.   Frankel, *Democratic Prospect*, 167.

20.   Ibid., 168.

21.   Ibid., 170.

22.   Ibid., 171.

23. Ibid., 176.

24. Carl J. Friedrich, *The New Belief in the Common Man* (Boston: Little, Brown & Co., 1942), 113.

25. Ibid., 5-6.

5

THE NEWEST POLL

THERE IS NO nation on earth which worships the idol of public opinion as does the United States. Americans are forever polling and being polled. Americans have even been known to do a poll on the results of a poll; in the fall of 1984, ABC asked viewers to call and voice an opinion on whether the poll of football coaches was correct in selecting Brigham Young University as the number one college team. So ingrained in the American psyche is polling, that one's opinion forever seems to be placed in the context of the majority's.

Many journalists have noted that American presidential campaigns are no longer races to be won or lost on election day, but are continuous. Weekly polls (sometimes daily polls) inform the public who is ahead on a day-to-day basis. Often the leading political story is not what candidate A says about candidate B or candidate B's countercharges, but how each is doing in the polls compared to the week before. How the propensity for updating elections has affected the electoral process is not clear. Obviously, the suspense and mystery of election night has vanished. The election has become just another poll. Whether candidates leading in pre-election polls would be more aggressive if they were unaware of their standing or whether those behind would be more conservative in their campaigns is speculation at best. Nor can it be determined if voters and campaign contributors would behave differently, if it were not for the polls.

What is clear is that professional polling has been thoroughly assimilated into the political process, starting with the first political poll, said to have been conducted by the *Natchez Courier* in an 1851 Tennessee election. Reporters interviewed eight hundred people and accurately predicted the outcome in fifteen of seventeen counties and the popular vote within two percentage points. The astounding accuracy of polls continues to the present. Politicians generally accept polls as a matter of faith. In 1980, politicians spent $20 million for some two thousand opinion polls. Polling as a campaign expenditure now ranks with advertising. "Polls have no measurable effect on voters," said columnist Jules Witcover, "but I've never met a politician who didn't believe they did."[1]

As Thomas Jefferson said in a letter to John Jay, it is "the duty of those entrusted with the administration of [public] affairs to conform themselves to the decided choice of their constituents." While campaigning for the Illinois legislature in 1836, Lincoln said that "acting as their [the people's] representative, I shall be governed by their will on all subjects upon which I have the means of knowing what their will is." Was the leadership of Jefferson and Lincoln diminished by their apparent desire to know what *the people* think? Did they lose independence, political fortitude, backbone? It could be said that the methods of ascertaining public opinion in their day were so primitive that as politicians Jefferson and Lincoln were immune from blindly conforming to public will. President Lyndon Johnson carried data on his job performance in his pocket. Could that be the reason he appeared so tortured towards the end of his presidency, with public acceptance of the Vietnam war declining? Historians say the test of leadership is the ability to stick to one's moral convictions in the face of public opinion. With polling having become a science, is it possible today for leaders to pursue conviction over popularity? Future presidents are likely to be creatures of the poll. Having risen in the political ranks by polling, the president of the future may find public approval as the ultimate end of political power.

This debate is as old as the Republic. In *The Federalist Papers*, Alexander Hamilton warned that the administration of public affairs "does not require an unqualified compliance to every sudden breeze of passion, or every transient impulse [from the people]."[2] Winston Churchill admonished that "Nothing is more dangerous than to live in the temperamental atmosphere of a Gallup poll, always taking one's temperature . . . there is only one duty, only one safe course, and that is to be right and not to fear to do or say what you believe to be right."

The American representative system attempted to give leaders the longest possible leash from the sway of passion and public opinion. Leadership was dispersed among the states and federal government. Power was distributed among the various branches. Madison and Hamilton thought politicians would be popular by being right, but they could not be right solely by being popular.

The long-standing national phobia over the unfettered rule of public opinion has been documented in every generation. The candidate who wants to know which issue will play before which audience "constitutes a politics without vision in which the blind lead the blind."[4] It is lethal for politicans to consult polls rather than their consciences.

In truth, American political thought has never fully escaped the long, historic shadow of the masses as rabble and the majority as a tyrant. Of all the shortcomings of democracy, de Tocqueville most feared democratic rule run wild: "I hold it to be an impious and detestable maxim that, politically speaking, the people have a right to do anything. . . . I think liberty is endangered when this power [majority rule] finds no obstacle which can retard its course. . . ."[5]

Later in the nineteenth century, Englishman James Bryce observed the same qualities in American political life. What de Tocqueville dubbed the tyranny of the majority, Bryce called the "fatalism of the multitude." Fearing unfettered majority power, Bryce wrote, "He whom the multitude condemns or ignores has no further court of appeal to look to."[6] In the American politician, Bryce saw someone constantly afraid to commit himself lest he cross majority will: "The belief in the right of the majority lies very near the belief that the majority is right."[7]

One can only imagine what a de Tocqueville or Bryce would say about video voting. Probably they would agree that video voting is both totally American and thoroughly obnoxious. In this view, if public opinion polls seem dangerous, then at-home video voting is surely disastrous.

Most theorists could accept video voting itself if it were a mere substitute for voting at polls. Few would object if the handicapped, the elderly, or the parent at home with young children exercised his franchise via the TV screen, predicated, of course, on a technically verifiable system of voter identification being installed in the home terminal. Such a system of voting is no more significant than an electronic absentee ballot.

The concern arises when the same technology is used for *issue sampling*. Rather than a Gallup, Harris, or Yankelovich randomly calling several hundred people, pollsters and politicians could ask for a mass poll by means of the screen. This would not be a random sample, but a mass sample. Has America stumbled into a "de facto" direct democracy?

Hypothetically, each congressman could have a terminal in his office and when an issue came up, he would sample constituent opinion. How about the B-1 bomber or the MX missile? If the vote is 80 to 20 in favor of the B-1 and 80 to 20 opposed to the MX, the congressman would seemingly vote for the B-1 and reject the MX. He would likely disregard all the briefings by defense officials, information provided by lobbyists, and congressional debate itself. Perhaps the vote among the constituency would be excruciatingly close. At that point, does the congressman allow ambiguity to give him true legislative freedom or does he still feel bound to vote with the will of the majority?

A most sophisticated system would allow the legislator to determine who is pushing the buttons. He would know if the votes came from a section of the district whose economy is dependent on a defense industry. He would know basic demographics: are the homes in an affluent neighborhood; a Catholic one; do most people have college educations; are they Republicans? If, in fact, the politician had the same access as the cable provider, he would know how specific constituents voted on every issue—a possibility that raises a grave privacy question.

Truly, legislators relying on daily constituent feedback would become puppets of the polls. They would have abandoned all pretense of political independence.

The technology exists to take the legislative branches of government—Congress, state legislatures, local councils—to that extreme. The inclination to poll the public on everything predisposes politicians to use the system in the name of constituent service. It is, of course, not service, but abdication of legal and moral responsibility. Even before politicians have the ease of tapping into a computer bank, polls on issues are far too prevalent. The exquisite pleasure politicians receive when their votes are in congruence with the will of the majority signals trouble ahead when a technology is in place which provides the legislator immediate information and gratification.

When politicians begin to use the system in such a fashion, the technology will have been thoroughly perverted. Special interest groups will mobilize mass telephone and direct mail campaigns intended to have their supporters register opinions with legislators investigating public opinion. The mass mailing of post cards to congressmen to support or reject certain legislation is standard practice. These campaigns would be amateurish by comparison to an orchestrated video vote.

The most diligent legislator would be baffled by a video vote. He might know who is voting, but would not know whether the thought behind the vote was independent or part of a national effort to rig the opinion sample. To that extent, traditional random samples are more accurate.

A whole new industry would evolve. Billboards exhorting members of Planned Parenthood to stand by their terminals at seven Friday evening, when a vote on birth control funding was scheduled, would appear. Radio commercials by labor urging union members to register electronically an opinion on the minimum wage would fill the airwaves just prior to a congressional vote. Direct mailings would be sent daily to members of all interest groups giving the time when policy relevant to their interest would be up for a video vote.

What is depicted here is a gross caricature of an American political system swallowing a technology whole. It's a warning. A society emotionally tied to following the majority and in possession of the technical capability to measure mass opinions can become a victim of its own inquisitiveness.

The use of video voting on an issue-by-issue basis would surely destroy the representative system of government. Pluralism, as envisioned by the Founding Fathers, requires limiting the number of participants in policy struggles. Most people, in fact, do not have strong opinions on issues. They vote for and against candidates, but leave specific policy decisions to the elected leaders. For most of us, politics is a peripheral concern. In one survey, for example, people were asked what laws they would pass if they were elected to Congress. Incredibly, almost half of those questioned, some 47 percent, had no opinion. Only 22 percent could name a single issue which motivated them to vote for a particular candidate for Congress.[8] For 63 percent of the population, voting is their only political activity. Fewer than 9 percent ever wear a political campaign button, place a bumper sticker on a car, or attend a political rally. Only 7 percent ever work for a political party and a mere 5 percent say they are members of a political club.[9]

According to congressmen who send questionnaires to constituents, only 14 percent of the voters bother to fill out and return the surveys.[10] Robert Dahl's renowned work *Who Governs?* notes that only 13 percent of the people he studied in New Haven had *ever* been active in terms of a local political issue. Furthermore, only 16 percent had any contact with a local political official.[11]

Sometimes in America, it seems that the engine of democracy chugs along on one piston.

The system has functioned as well as it has because of the indifference of some, but also because representative government understands vested interests. Theoretically, in the American system, no one feels that government has abandoned him, though there are, of course, millions of powerless, the unrepresented. Each group's most fundamental concern is sacrosanct. So in Congress, no important bloc loses on a policy question affecting its very survival. In the nineteenth century, John C. Calhoun called it the concept of the concurrent majority. His belief was that on most issues all groups would gladly compromise as long as that group was assured that its most vital interest would be protected.

Calhoun's concurrent majority is unworkable when legislators look first to what the numerical majority says.

Even the most cursory consideration of the effect of video voting upon the representative system of government now existing on the national, state, and local levels indicates that the very foundation of the system would be threatened by placing issue voting in the constituents' hands. All the dangers of majority rule, which have long been the topic of the theorists, would become reality.

Direct voting is not merely a question of overdosing on democracy. It represents the mixing of two inherently incompatible political systems. Direct democracy is not additional indirect democracy—more representative government—it is an entirely *different* species. Direct democracy can work, but it cannot be grafted onto a representative system.

Direct democracy must stand alone; by definition it is simply impossible to intertwine direct and indirect democracy, two discrete branches of the tree of democracy. If experimentation with video voting on public issues fails, it can be attributed to misapplication. Opinion surveys through interactive cable or a two-way computer network are dangerous only when elected leaders take their cues from the terminal screen. For reasons which will be explained later, rational, local government can be designed to take advantage of the new interactive technology, keeping in mind the significant difference between video voting and video democracy.

Any discussion of the political ramifications of the new technology should begin with a look at political participation. After all, democracy is based on the assumption that citizens, when asked to contribute opinions, will do so with intelligence and understanding.[12]

Contemporary sociological research seems to support the position that representative government values nonparticipation (although the mythology of representative government would say the opposite). Direct democracy values mass participation in theory and fact. Representative democracy functions best in an atmosphere of consensus on basic values. Not everyone has to be an active participant as long as his fundamental interests are protected. The belief that politics is not the most noble of professions serves indirect democracy well. As studies indicate, there is great virtue to limiting participation, as long as the nonparticipants believe their interests are being served.

One-third of all Americans are totally apathetic to the political world. These people are utterly blind to all but the most cataclysmic and publicized political events. Sixty percent of the population are spectators who observe and upon occasion vote, but stay removed from the political fray. In the purest sense, a scant 2 percent are routinely involved in politics.[13]

Of course, people float in and out of the political mainstream depending on the issue. The person with intense feelings on abortion will be at home pushing buttons when the moment to vote arrives. But a week later, the same individual will be golfing rather than participating in the vote on how to spend the budget surplus. When it comes to political participation, people tune in and out as if they were sampling music on various radio stations. If the issue has appeal, then the person might become more informed and even write a letter to a congressman or city councilman. If the issue appears uninteresting or seems to affect someone else, the average American leaves politics to the politician.

In Herbert Gans's classic study of suburbia, *The Levittowners*, people are pleasingly apolitical. Although voters have the power to terminate a politician's career abruptly, few think much about elections. To the average Levittowner, politics is for the politicians, who, once elected, strive to keep public disagreement to a minimum and are quite content to hold the public at a distance. The latter is not hard to achieve, since only a handful of citizens bother to attend public meetings. Feedback comes from the few who are angered by governmental decisions. It is not that the people simply don't care what government does. Government activity does not touch most lives and there is a natural reluctance to communicate with public officials.

In Levittown, as elsewhere, the politician is wedged between two opposing ideas on every major issue—with the majority of the community silent as usual. It is not surprising that the politicians Gans studied avoided constituent contact. The only reasonable way a political figure can cope with the special interests and the few citizens who bother to speak out is to keep a very low profile. In such an environment, the brokering of vested interests can best be accomplished. As Gans put it: "Government must develop institutional means to shield itself from the citizens."[14] The politician seeks an equilibrium that preserves the status quo and, of course, the retention of political power.

Levittown is ethnically diverse, with large numbers of Catholics and Jews. Most residents are from lower middle-class backgrounds. The majority has completed high school and a large proportion has attended some college. They grumble continually about politics, but rarely act. Their overriding concerns center on family, job, child rearing, and the like.

Gans observes that politicians in Levittown rely on the public hearing to keep the lid on conflict and thus maintain power. The politicos, the author states, devise two governments—the real and the performance. The real goes on behind closed doors and the performance takes place at public hearings. The hearings are true to the most altruistic assumptions about democratic local government, but the decisions have been made backstage. The charade allows government to function normally, but gives the impression that democracy is at work:

Ultimately, all suggestions for improvement [of local government] require greater political participation, and this solution is illusory. . . .Politicization would be best achieved if people were required to participate more directly and actively in politics—but this process requires drastic reorganization of government, and of the government-citizen relationship, which is not likely to happen.[15]

The Levittown system is very neat, very clean, very antiseptic and very undemocratic. The shadow government works behind the scenes balancing interests, keeping the handful of interested citizens content. The obvious goal is to mute conflict, because smooth political waters assure reelection for the politicians. The voters go along with the sham because they have little interest in participating themselves, but want to sustain the *appearance* of participatory democracy. Everyone is satisfied—the politicians, the special interests, and the general public.

It should be abundantly clear that the Levittown system could never survive input from video voting. The political backroom where interests are juggled cannot be reconciled when exposed by the harsh glare of public opinion polls. A politician cannot hide behind the appearance of consensus, when a TV screen indicates that he is in a minority. Public exposure strikes at the very core of Levittown's consensus politics. As was the case in the example of video voting posited for Congress, instant public opinion on the local level is of equally dubious value. A politician can only serve one master. Will he be accountable to his colleagues or the video voters? In a representative system, mass participation is of secondary importance to a high level of general satisfaction.

Because the success of true direct democracy is contingent upon mass participation, the representative system requires passive acceptance of the political status quo. Reflecting upon a sociological study of a mid-Atlantic community with the mythical name of Eastport, it becomes even clearer that participation is a nonessential political value. The residents of Eastport who were interviewed in the study were a roofer, a drill press operator, and a salesman, all the very symbol of middle America in material standing, moral values, and political attitudes. Each demonstrates a strong sense of equality: "I'm as good as anybody else. The rich guy, just because he's got money, is no better than I am."[16] And yet they are outside the political system. They accept the frailties of popular government "with eyes open." The citizens of Eastport are not involved in government. A few may have written to a congressman and fewer still have ever attempted to organize a petition drive. "The fact is that these men were pretty discouraged by the idea of *doing* something about any big problem."[17]

Although the men of Eastport were noninvolved, they, like most Americans, believe government is basically just and benign. They disassociate themselves from politics and still function quite well in their daily lives. The study concludes that the politically uninvolved of Eastport accept as a matter of faith that government is looking out for them.

In Dahl's classic study of political power in New Haven it was found that most citizens participate only occasionally, then revert to their previous state of inactivity. A small group of professional politicians and the politically aware composed the dominant power group. "If the pluralist system was very far from being an oligarchy, it was also a long way from achieving the goal of political equality advocated by the philosophers of democracy."[18] Dahl acknowledged that the political strata could be penetrated by anyone with the inclination to do so, but few people bothered. The lives of most people in New Haven revolved around food, sex, love, family, work, play, shelter, and comfort—not politics.[19] Dahl found that only half of those registered to vote ever talked about politics and local governmental affairs. People assumed that the political professionals were minding the government store. Dahl discovered that democracy, as it is presented in theory, did not exist in New Haven. "The inescapable fact is that those who write about politics are deeply concerned about public affairs and sometimes find it difficult to believe most other people are not. . . . Whether or not the myth was reality in Athens will probably never be known."[20]

It appears that in a representative system, where people are not asked to make daily decisions, political participation is self-limiting. What is not clear is whether people fail to participate because the system does not encourage participation or fail to participate because politics is boring and unrewarding. The guess here is that for a large segment of the population, the answer is the former.

V. O. Key, Jr. spoke of a thin layer of people highly active in politics; a thicker layer of those who did sporadic campaigning or talked about politics, and an extremely thick layer of the politically inert.[21] Key theorized that people who participate in the more active forms of politics also participate in the less active forms.[22] If a person electioneers for a candidate, he is very likely to attend party meetings; if he attends party meetings, he is sure to be in contact with elected officials; if he is in contact with elected officials, he undoubtedly places bumper stickers on his car; if he places bumper stickers on his car, he definitely votes in primaries; if he votes in primaries, he also votes in general elections. It is a one-way relationship moving from more to less active.

There are some predictors of a person's likelihood to be politically active. Studies indicate that the better educated a person is, the more likely he is to participate in politics. In 1964, for example, 81 percent of the people with some college education voted, compared to 62 percent of those with grade school education.[23] As a general rule, the higher the socioeconomic status, especially education, the more likely a person is to be active in politics. People who identify with a political party, who belong to a labor union, or who understand the intricacies of the political system are among the most likely to be active. Several psychological tests for political activity exist: people who are effective in everyday life are more inclined to participate, while people who are anxious and consumed by personal problems are less likely to be involved. "The chaotic, rough-and-tumble environment of competitive politics carries few rewards for the thin-skinned, neurotic personalities. . . . The political arena is not a hospitable place for the insecure, timid and withdrawn people."[24]

The commodities of participation in the age of representative democracy include money and leisure time. Money is the life-blood of campaigns. He who contributes can gain access and influence. Further, on a practical level, active participants need leisure time to attend meetings and rallies and to electioneer. For the poor, even money for a babysitter may tip the scales in favor of nonparticipation. In fact, only 10 percent of the electorate contribute to campaigns,[25] a fact supporting the notion that representative democracy restricts participation. Politics has traditionally been the sport of the well-to-do. By its very nature, representative government makes political participation into an exclusive club, of sorts. Dahl found that the higher the income, the greater the participation. In the lowest economic group 82 percent were highly inactive while 4 percent were highly active. In the highest income group 42 percent were highly inactive, but 38 percent were highly active. Under the present system, money and political activism strongly correlate.[26]

Representative democracy encourages the formation of a political elite whose members are generally people of both means and status. While each individual may not actively participate in every policy debate or in every election, there is a core group that contributes campaign money; shows up for council meetings; writes letters to the editors; electioneers; talks to friends and neighbors about public affairs and, above all, informs itself about public issues.

It is not so much that the other 80 percent or so of the population has abdicated civic responsibility, but that the system is so complex that it demands a special effort to be involved. Central to the representative system are candidates, interest groups, and political parties. As yet, one cannot just flip on a TV and participate. Money, leisure time, social status, and psychological stability are necessary resources. Representative government limits the players, while giving lip service to mass participation. If there is any American consensus, it is that there exists a political caste—as long as that caste does not challenge basic values the system will be allowed to perpetuate itself.

One fallacy is that the political caste possesses an unusual degree of merit. "In America today, men of affairs are not so much dogmatic as they are mindless. . . . The elite of power, wealth and celebrity are not the elite of culture, knowledge and sensibility."[27] Americans bow to the cult of the expert, the specialist. Some have said that the expert is more problem than solution. As President Kennedy said after the disastrous Bay of Pigs invasion, "I should have known better than to listen to experts."

Americans *assume* policy is complex, inaccessible to the common man. There is, to be sure, a difference between technical decisions and logical policy. Is a traffic engineer needed to determine if a major highway should be built? Certainly the engineer is needed to provide the *facts* on how many vehicles would travel the road, how many lanes it should have, and how many exits should be built. But given the facts, is not the common man capable of deciding overall policy,—i.e., should the road be built at all? To turn over such a decision to consultants—bureaucrats and a political elite—fails to advance effective democracy. And, unfortunately, it can well fail to provide the correct policy decision. As one commentator observes, "It is not that experts mean to mislead. But [their interests are] theories, jealousies and a yen to say what the listener wants to hear. When what you need is common sense, you get only expertise."[28]

Pure direct democracy is incompatible with political elitism. When the people have direct impact on policy the necessity of a special political caste dissolves. The many affectations of representative democracy—money, interest groups, election campaigns, experts— become less important, if not totally superfluous.

The great flaw in recent discussion of direct democracy is that it has invariably been construed as an adjunct—an add-on—to indirect democracy. Such a concept creates an entity possessing the worst aspects of both. The value of representative democracy is leadership and resolution of conflict. The value of direct democracy is mass participation and citizen self-worth. Indirect and direct democracy cannot form a harmonious union simply because the word *democracy* is common to both; they are very different systems with unique strengths and weaknesses.

Notes

1.   Jules Witcover, "Can We Believe the Pollsters?" *The Reporter* 38, no. 10 (May 16, 1968): 14.

2.   Charles W. Roll and Albert H. Cantril, *Polls: Their Use and Misuse in Politics* (Cabin John, Md.: Seven Locks Press, 1980), 137.

3.   Ibid., 136.

4.   Carey McWilliams, "Second Thoughts," *The Nation* 229, no. 20 (December 15, 1979): 615.

5.   Alexis de Tocqueville, *Democracy in America*, Henry Reeve Text, ed. Phillips Bradley (New York: Vintage Books, 1945), 1: 266.

6.   James Bryce, *The American Commonwealth* (New York: Macmillan, 1914) 2: 353.

7.   Ibid., 350.

8.   Robert S. Erikson and Norman R. Luttbeg, *American Public Opinion: Its Origins, Content and Impact* (New York, John Wiley & Sons, 1973), 2:

9.   Ibid., 5.

10. Ibid., 268.

11. Robert Dahl, *Who Governs?* (New Haven: Yale Univ. Press, 1961), 277.

12. George Gallup, "Pollsters, Not Prophets," *Society* 13, no. 6 (September/October, 1976): 22.

13. Lester W. Milbrath, *Political Participation* (Chicago: Rand McNally & Co., 1965), 21.

14. Herbert J. Gans, *The Levittowners* (New York: Pantheon, 1967), 309.

15. Ibid., 358-59.

16. Robert E. Lane, *Political Ideology* (New York: The Free Press, 1962), 67.

17. Ibid., 164.

18. Dahl, *Who Governs?* 86.

19. Ibid., 279.

20. Ibid., 280-81.

21. James David Barber, *Citizen Politics: An Introduction to Political Behavior* (Chicago: Markham Publishing, 1969), 9.

22. Ibid., 10.

23. Ibid., 11.

24. Milbrath, *Political Participation*, 88-89.

25. Ibid., 19.

26. Dahl, *Who Governs?* 283.

27. C. Wright Mills, *Power, Politics and People* (New York: Oxford Univ. Press, 1963), 605-10.

28. Richard A. Snyder, "Democracy's Ills and Cures," *Vital Speeches* 48, no. 21 (August 15, 1982): 690.

6

PARTY, POLITICS, AND TECHNOLOGY

LIKE THE DOCTRINAIRE Marxist who forever anticipates the withering away of the state, so American political historians are forever waiting for a realigning election. That's an election where party loyalty swings decisively from one party to another and that party remains dominant for a generation.

It is a virtual consensus among historians and political scientists that there is cyclical unity to American politics. The theory is that there is a rhythm to realigning elections which seem to occur every twenty-eight to thirty-six years. They call it the cycle of party realignment.

The theory goes like this: American political history moves in a circle. Toward the end of each cycle the issues become clouded and confused. The old parties offer old rhetoric and old solutions to new national problems. Voters, who are largely discontented, see little difference between the two national parties, and third parties rise up to challenge existing political powers. Finally, a cataclysmic or tension-producing event occurs, which causes the break-up of the old parties. Following the upheaval, a long period of political stability begins again. A new majority party emerges and retains power until the forces of realignment begin to build some thirty years later. The cycle of discontent, third-party challenge, crisis, and rebuilding begins once more. More than one historian has called the cycle of realignment "America's surrogate for revolution."[1]

Observers of American political history describe five realigning elections. There is great dispute over whether the election of Richard Nixon in 1968 signaled the end of FDR's Democratic coalition on the national level. The verdict is clouded by two factors. In 1972, Nixon was reelected in a landslide over Democrat George McGovern. That, in itself, might support the thesis that 1968 was a realigning election. However, four years later Democrat Jimmy Carter defeated Nixon's second vice-president, Gerald Ford. The Watergate scandal, which forced Nixon to resign in disgrace in 1974, obviously weighed heavily on the 1976 campaign. Secondly, Democrats nominated a Southerner for the first time since the Civil War. The South, which had been steadily turning Republican for a generation, swung back into the Democratic column. In subsequent presidential elections in 1980 and 1984, the Republican, Ronald Reagan, won enormous victories, the latter being one of the most crushing defeats the Democratic party has ever received. Is it fair to conclude that if it were not for Watergate and the nomination of a Democratic Southerner, the Republicans would have completed a political cycle of realignment? No one may ever know. It is at least defensible to say that the Republicans were certainly on the edge of concluding a realignment when the Watergate burst. Whether it has been consummated to date is not readily apparent.

As we will discover, 1968 was *the* TV election. Historians were expecting realignment, but may have stumbled upon something entirely different—the beginnings of *dealignment*. By 1968, voters were well on their way toward transcending party labels. The individual candidate, not the party, was the consequence of TV politics. Parties might use television, but television could (and has) damaged party loyalty to an extent not yet measured. Dealignment may have been the ultimate gift to politics from the mass medium called television.

Let's look at 1968, but also at the five true watershed elections. The argument will be made here that realigning elections can not only be predicted and understood not only in the context of the ebb and flow of parties, but also in terms of communications technology. Advances in communications obviously are not the sole cause of political realignment. Yet it is necessary to point out the relationship between communications and realignment.

The relationship is not strange at all. Politics has always used available communications technology. Eighteenth-century politicians would have been familiar with public addresses, broadsheets, pamphlets, and pulpit oratory as means of communicating with the public. The underlying fact is this: *Every technological change in communications also changes politics.* There is, of course, a lag between invention and eventual political impact. Technology must be adapted to political use. Nevertheless, all winning candidates in American realigning elections employed the most modern and sophisticated communications technology available. The import of this relationship between politics and developing technology cannot be understated. America is on the threshold of a new communications technology—interactive television. Political thinkers who confine their research to voting blocs and demographics miss the point. Look ahead at the newest communications technology. See how it will be used in the political process and project that use into partisan politics.

But first, a glance back over the pattern of realigning elections:

—The election of Jefferson in 1800, ending the dominance of the Federalist party.

—The election of Jackson in 1828, ending the rule of the Jeffersonian-Republicans and beginning the dominance of frontier Democracy which would continue in power with few exceptions until the Civil War.

—The election of Lincoln in 1860, inaugurating an era of Republican dominance which, with minor exceptions, lasted through the nineteenth and into the twentieth century.

—The election of McKinley in 1896, which is seen as a victory of post-Civil War industrialism over insurgent agrarianism.

—The election of Franklin Roosevelt in 1932, which terminated laissez-faire Republican rule and instituted welfare state liberalism.[2]

With near computer precision, historians can match the facts leading up to those five elections with the theory of cyclical realignment. In all cases, the voices of the dominant parties grew stale; the public became discontent; third parties sprouted to fill the leadership voids; a powerful event shook the system, and a critical realigning election occurred. Then a new party constructed a dominant coalition, only to be washed away in time by the historic tide.

The election of Jefferson in 1800 does not fit neatly into the mold. Mass communication was virtually as primitive as it was when Washington took office. The message of Jefferson's election was that a genuine two-party system could take root; ideology could change; power could be transferred, all without plunging the nation into political catastrophe. Eighteen hundred was a realigning election only in the context that political power changed hands. At that early date in the nation's history, there was no political history to speak of; therefore it is difficult to fit the theoretical frame of cyclical realignment and the 1800 election together.

Until the 1830s, newspapers were not media of mass communication. First of all, they were not mass. In larger cities there were many papers, most of which were weeklies. Very few had circulations more than several hundred readers. In 1810, for example, a New York daily had nine hundred subscribers and that was considered large. Secondly, newspapers communicated information, but not news. Reports in the early nineteenth-century papers consisted mainly of business transactions, government reports, and letters of European events that were usually several months old when the paper was published. The papers were written for a mercantile and political elite. The writers were printers, not journalists. Their intent was advertising, not news. No effort was made to reach a general readership. Even if the intent was there, it was technologically impossible to print a mass circulation paper. Every broadsheet had to be pressed by human muscle power. In addition, typesetting was especially tedious work and the newsprint itself was extraordinarily expensive.

For these reasons it would be unfair to attribute the advent of Jeffersonian-Republicanism and Jackson's frontier democracy to changes in the media. Newspapers in the early nineteenth century were similar to what would be called political newsletters today. Papers took a political point of view, played favorites, and wrote for a select group of insiders. Both the Federalists and the Republicans had their own cadre of favorite editors and papers, and they were well rewarded for toeing the party line.

The subsequent realigning elections, however, are clearly characterized by strong involvement of media. Technology advanced rapidly in the first third of the nineteenth century and, as a result, the nation entered into an era of mass communications. It can be said that mass communications became the midwife to the birth of mass politics.

Advances in technology brought with them changes in communications. In 1799, a paper-making machine was patented, resulting in comparatively inexpensive, accessible newsprint. Fourteen years later, George Clymer of Philadelphia invented the Columbian press, which abandoned the ancient principle of pressing pages by physically twisting a screw. Instead, Clymer's press relied on pressure applied by a series of levers. A few years later, the newspaper industry adopted the steam-driven cylinder press, which was nothing shy of revolutionary. By 1832, a double cylinder press had the capacity of printing four thousand papers an hour. Circulations rose accordingly. Eighteen thirty-five saw the *New York Sun* selling eight thousand one-cent copies daily. The day of the penny press had arrived.

With the ability to print a mass circulation paper, the *New York Sun* pioneered a style which won over the general public and was copied throughout the nation. The *Sun* broke with tradition and decided to print whatever was readable and interesting regardless of how important it was to the politicians and business community. On July 4, 1834, the *Sun* sent a reporter to copy the police blotter: "Bill Doty got drunk because he had horrors so bad he couldn't keep sober. Committed."[3] Here's another example: "Sudden death—Ann McDonough, of Washington Street, attempted to drink a pint of rum on a wager, on Wednesday afternoon last. Before it was half swallowed, Ann was a corpse. Served her right." In the 1830s, The *New York Herald* (which had begun to compete with the *Sun*) tripled its circulation during the trial of a man who allegedly murdered a prostitute. The defendant, a young clerk named Robinson, was the first nonprominent person to achieve such fame. More importantly for him, he was acquitted. The formula hasn't changed much since the 1830s. The *National Enquirer, People Magazine,* and the television show "Real People" can all trace their ancestry to the penny press of the 1830s. Gossip, sex, violence—it became news when the papers said so. A generation later when the nation would face the most divisive and profound of issues, the newspapers already had an audience.

At the time this development was a revelation, a thunderbolt. Newspapers had power. The ability to talk to thousands upon thousands at one time had never existed in all of human history. Before, communication was restricted to the distance a man's voice would carry and by the technological restrictions of printing. By the 1830s, those barriers had been overcome. James Gordon Bennett, founder of the *New York Herald,* proclaimed a new dawn on August 19, 1836: "A newspaper can be made to take the lead of all these in the great movements of human thought and human civilization. A newspaper can send more souls to heaven, and save more from hell, than all the churches or chapels in New York—besides making money at the same time. Let it be tried."[4]

Shortly thereafter, the invention of the telegraph reduced space to the speed of electric current. News became just that—news. After several years of experimentation, Congress appropriated $30,000 to build a telegraph line between Washington and Baltimore. On Friday, May 24, 1844, with the Democratic convention meeting in Baltimore, the first political news was disseminated by telegraph. As one observer exclaimed, "This is indeed the annihilation of space." Coupled with the telegraph, the inventions of the steamship and steam locomotive radically changed communications in the brief period from the election of Jackson to the nomination of Democrat James K. Polk in 1844.

America was also vastly different politically from what it was when Old Hickory was elected. The nation had become intensely partisan. The Whigs and the Democrats had matured into well-organized, stable political parties. The 1830s was also the decade when suffrage was given to all white males. In twelve short years from 1828 to 1840, the turnout in national elections had grown from 1.1 to 17 million. Parties held torchlight parades, barbecues, raised money, and had well-disciplined committees in all counties and towns. "Men proudly carried party labels and loyalties to the edge of the grave. Party regularity was a virtue, straight ticket voting was a political duty of every good man, and switching from party to party was condemned as a vice."[5]

It was in this period of broadbased political parties and fierce loyalties that the general circulation newspapers began to tackle an issue of far greater import than local pickpockets and neighborhood drunks. That issue was slavery. Newspaper historians credit *New York Tribune* editor Horace Greeley with doing more to crystallize Northern opinion on the slavery issue than any single individual. His contribution to the history of mass opinion formation is no less astounding. Prior to the Civil War, Greeley's daily paper had a circulation of 50,000, and his nationally distributed weekly paper went to 200,000 subscribers. Headlines like the following were indicative of Greeley's *Tribune*: "A Scene of Cruelty and Bloodshed; Facts of Slavery; The Shame of Virginia."

"With gusto the data presented savage executions of slaves and exhibited mulattos running from the dripping jaws of bloodhounds. It was never heavy reading, and was often spiced with sexual atrocities."[6] Two generations later historian James Ford Rhodes advised readers of the *Atlantic Monthly* to study the weekly *Tribune* to understand what motivated the 1.8 million Lincoln voters in 1860. Other Northern newspapers wrote passionately against the South's peculiar institution in the years leading up to the war, but few as crusadingly as the *Tribune*. On the opposite side of the Mason-Dixon Line, newspapers lashed out at the Northern abolitionists.

Numerous brilliant minds have dedicated their careers to comprehending the dissolution of the Union in 1860. Theories abound. Why did the election of 1860 become a realigning election and lead directly to the outbreak of war? All the necessary elements were there. The old parties were fading, their rhetoric failing to meet the greatest challenge of the age. In 1856, the Whigs did not nominate a candidate for president, even though four years previously the Whig candidate, Winfield Scott, only narrowly lost the popular vote. Southerners captured the soul of the Democratic party in the 1850s. In 1860, pro-slavery forces bolted from the Democratic party, even though the nominee, Stephen Douglas, had already given in to them. Temperate and moderate voters had few options by 1860. Just as the theory of realignment posits, minor parties such as the Know Nothings, Free Soilers, and the Liberty party struggled over the corpses of the rapidly disintegrating Whig and Democratic parties. The upstart, but sectional, Republicans would begin a long ascendancy with Lincoln's election.

The requisite incendiary issues were also present. There was Stephen Douglas's Nebraska Bill of 1854, which extended state's rights to the west, allowing for the people to decide if a state was to be free or slave. The Nebraska Bill effectively repealed Henry Clay's 1820 compromise, which had set a northern boundary on slavery.[7] The Dred Scott decision coming from a Southern-dominated court also served as kindling for the fires of political upheaval.

There are as many theories of causes of the Civil War as there are historians. Some speak of the effect of immigration or industrialization or the demands for homesteads or federal aid for harbors and rivers. The consensus, of course, is that the issue of slavery and the failure of the existing parties to deal with that most politically treacherous issue ultimately led to the fateful election of 1860.

What must also be remembered is that the 1860 election was the first realigning election where the mass media played a significant role. The Civil War would likely have occurred had there been no newspapers at all. Yet, for the first time in history, millions felt as if they were direct participants in the drama unfolding in the Congress, the Supreme Court, and in the western territories. No one could deny that the masses in the North and South had the right to hear or be heard. The telegraph and the modern printing presses left little time for sober reflection on the events of the day. News was written and read in a hurry. The young but already influential communications industry helped polarize the nation. In doing so, the press of the mid-nineteenth century may have nudged the country over the precipice of debate into the ravine of war.

By 1896, the political wheel had made another complete turn. Another realigning election was at hand. Although the Republicans controlled the White House through most of the post-Civil War era, the political system was essentially balanced and competitive. The Republicans were strongest in the East and West. Until the 1890s, a tacit understanding held that the goal of the nation was to rebuild from the ravages of the Civil War. Raw, unregulated industrialism was the order of the day. Whether it was the mammouth railroad industry, the fledgling oil and steel industries, or the ever-growing communications industry, the nation was content with business as usual.

With both parties deferring to the industrial elites, two major groups—farmers and the urban working class—were left without representation. In times of prosperity the forgotten millions could survive, but the 1890s sorely tested the economic system and those who were left out demanded to be let in. Cleveland's second term was a national disaster. Unemployment rose to frightening heights. Financial panic, business failures, and desperate strikes were rampant.[8] As in the years immediately preceding the Civil War, sectional strife proved troublesome and divisive as the rural west and south joined hands to fight the financial clout of the east.

As happens before a realigning election, minor parties arose to fill the void left by the spiritually bankrupt major parties. In 1892, the Populist or People's party was born. It nominated James Weaver for president that year and won more than a million votes. The Populists stood for an eight-hour day, a graduated income tax, public ownership of railroads and other utilities, direct election of senators, and a regulated economy.[9] Populism was essentially a rural party unable to bridge its differences with organized labor. In retrospect Populism initiated a slow but constant philosophic shift in the Democratic party.

In 1896, the Democrats nominated William Jennings Bryan, the then young Nebraskan who had close emotional ties with the Populists. The Republicans countered with William McKinley, who was much at home with the eastern business elite. It would be a viciously contested election with clear-cut differences between the candidates. It was not uncommon for factory owners to warn their employees not to report for work if Bryan won the election. For his part, Bryan was quoted as calling New York "the enemy's country." With Bryan favoring the free coinage of silver, Democrats in the north split from their party's nominee and did their best to defeat the westerner. When the votes were counted, McKinley had taken every northern state east of the Mississippi River, including every county in New England. But Bryan and his fanatical supporters had won the hearts and votes of the west and the south.

Historians look to 1896 as a realigning election because it drove the Democratic party into a generation-long slumber in the North. The brief exception to that statement was the Democratic resurgence between 1910 and 1916.[10] Yet there was in Bryan's defeat a clue to the bright future of the Democratic party, which would be snatched up by Franklin Roosevelt. Bryan spoke to America's disadvantaged—the urban working class, the farmers, the immigrants, the Negro, and the small businessman. In 1896, few of these groups were organized and prepared to seize the moment. With the eventual demise of the northeastern gold Democrats, a political vacuum was created. That void would be filled by urban labor and new immigrant groups who would take over the party in the northeast.

While the nation was playing out the final phases of the realigning cycle, momentous technological changes were infiltrating the communications industry. By the 1880s, natural gas provided light in many urban American homes, so that reading became an activity for the evening leisure hours. By the 1890s, Edison's dream of illuminating the nation with inexpensive incandescent light was becoming a reality. The American genius for invention was in its heyday in the latter part of the nineteenth century. Alexander Graham Bell's telephone revolutionized communication as well as the gathering and reporting of news. Somewhat less significant was the development of the typewriter, which gave speed and clarity to written communications. By 1885, newspaper presses could churn out 30,000 papers per hour, but the process of setting type by hand required slow meticulous work. Enter Ottmar Mergenthaler, the German-born naturalized American, who changed the printing industry forever. In 1886, Mergenthaler introduced the linotype machine, which did away with typesetting by hand. By bringing copper matrices into contact with a molten, fast-cooling alloy, type could be set by a printer sitting at a keyboard.

This technology allowed the newspaper to grow into a Leviathan.[11] The mid-1890s saw the *New York World*'s circulation grow to over a million copies a day. In 1892, only ten papers in the United States had circulations exceeding 100,000. Over the next 20 years the average newspaper doubled its circulation. With its immense reach, the newspaper would play a powerful role in the realigning election of 1896. The new technology so advanced newspapering that by 1914, there were 2,250 daily newspapers in the United States.

For newspaper buffs, the 1890s was a time to be treasured and studied. It was the day of the great newspaper wars between Joseph Pulitzer's *World* and William Randolph Hearst's *Journal*—a struggle mirrored by rival publishers throughout the country. It was a day of yellow journalism and intensely partisan newspapers. Above all, it was an era when newspapers reached the masses and what they said about politics was taken by readers as gospel.

In 1896, Hearst's *Journal* was the only newspaper in New York to endorse Bryan. Its publisher, who harbored his own presidential ambitions, gave the Democratic candidate $40,000 for his ill-fated campaign. Hearst's cartoonist, Homer Davenport, was at his best depicting McKinley's confidante Mark Hanna wearing dollar signs for clothing. On either side during the 1896 campaign, the word *objectivity* was rarely, if ever, spoken in newsrooms.

Bryan was lambasted from front page to last in most of the eastern press. The *New York Tribune* called him a "wretched, addle-pated boy posing in vapid vanity and mouthing resounding rottenness," and the *New York Post* associated the Democratic candidate with "the still surviving barbarism bred by slavery in the South and the reckless spirit of adventure in the mining camps of the west."[12] The *Philadelphia Press* attributed Bryan supporters with the "incarnate spirit of communism and anarchy."[13]

The political coverage in the American papers of the 1890s was a reflection of the competitive ethos of unleashed capitalism. It was also simply another aspect of the ongoing war for circulation which was applied to every edition of the late nineteenth-century newspaper. The magnates of the publishing industry gave readers drawings, cartoons, prizes, sensational stories, color Sunday supplements, and wide-ranging news coverage—all in a wild free-for-all to win circulation. The coverage of the Spanish American War was indicative of the competitive hysteria of the age. The *Journal* once published forty editions in one day. It chartered ten ships at a cost of $1,500 a day to bring news from Cuba to the mainland. Each of the major New York papers had five to twenty-five correspondents in the war zone. In just six months Hearst's *Journal* spent a half million dollars in its war coverage.

Would the Democratic party in the 1890s have staggered into impotence, if it were not for the daily newspapers perpetually attacking Bryan's agrarianism? Again, as in the Civil War period, the answer is probably yes. No one can question the extraordinary vitality and power of newspapers during this period. The papers certainly served to divide the nation into political camps and to squelch the voices of compromise. The 1896 election was depicted in both Democratic and Republican newspapers as a battle of good versus evil. Bryan's chances would have improved considerably if he had had the muscle of the press on his side. As it was, the press made the realignment virtually inevitable. Under any circumstance, given the posture of the press, returning to the competitive, but fairly placid state of American politics would have been impossible. The press made a fortune off political turmoil. The giant publishers who supported McKinley discovered that it was possible to bury the devil beneath stacks of newsprint. There was no going back. The cycle of American politics had swung again and it would be another thirty-six years before another realigning election would occur.

Before looking at the next realigning election, let's skip ahead for a moment to November 2, 1920. KDKA in Pittsburgh broadcast the results of the Warren Harding/James Cox election over a new contraption called radio. Only a comparative handful of people heard the historic broadcast, since there were less than a thousand commercial sets in the entire nation. Two years later there were 60,000 receivers and 400 radio stations in the United States. By 1924, there were three million radios. The number seemed to be multiplying geometrically, signalling an acceptance of a mass medium that was unparalleled in history. By 1933, thirty-three million sets were in American homes. In a very few years, an experiment in broadcasting had become an omnipresent force—an American institution. It brought New York concert halls to the backwoods; foreign news to the most provincial areas; information on new products to consumers, and, in very real terms, permanently transformed American politics.

The tremors of sweeping political change caused by the radio were felt by the ambitious governor of New York, Franklin Roosevelt. In January 1929, FDR spoke of the astounding reach of radio:

> Whereas five years ago ninety-nine out of one hundred people took their arguments from the editorials and news columns of the daily press, today at least half of the voters sitting at their own firesides listen to the actual words of the political leaders on both sides and make their decision on what they hear rather than what they read.[14]

Three years later Roosevelt would hitch an electoral revolution to the radio. His career and the fate of the nation would ride on the airwaves.

The Democratic party of the post-World War I era was an embryo of the party Roosevelt would lead in the 1930s. The previous realignment had split the Democrats into weak eastern and western wings. American politics was changing, but silently beneath the surface. Millions of European ethnics had swelled eastern and midwestern cities. The naturalized immigrants and their children found homes in the Democratic party. Industrial workers were by the 1920s beginning to organize in sufficient numbers to influence elections. Although still emotionally tied to the party of Lincoln, blacks outside the south were ripe to be picked by a party promising them a future other than second-class citizenship. At the same time, American colleges and universities were turning out greater numbers of graduates than ever before. While the ethnics, blue-collar workers, blacks, and intellectuals were finding acceptance in the Democratic party, the Republican party was mired in complacency and mediocrity. Its success in 1920 was attributed to a reaction to Wilson and a national desire to return to prewar values. But the Republicans had not changed much since McKinley's day. The Grand Old Party was not heeding the lessons of history and it would shortly fall victim to the rhythm of realignment.

Once again, as in the periods prior to 1860 and 1896, new third parties began to nudge the system as 1932 approached. Socialists were gaining converts; Sen. Huey P. Long was planning the Share Our Wealth Party and the radio priest from Royal Oak, Michigan, Charles Coughlin, was leading the National Union for Social Justice. Outsiders were sensing growing discontent and chipping away at the established parties.

The nation got a strong whiff of the future in the 1928 election, when Herbert Hoover defeated Al Smith. In much of rural America, Smith, the Democratic party's Catholic nominee, was terribly abused. The pastor of a large Oklahoma City Baptist congregation warned his parishioners, "If you vote for Al Smith, you're voting against Christ and you'll all be damned."[15]

Smith, a man with an eighth-grade education, won the votes of America's urban ethnics. In many eastern and midwestern cities, Irish, Jewish, and Polish ethnics gave Smith 70 to 80 percent of their votes. The foundation of Roosevelt's grand coalition had begun to crystallize.

A year later, the towering edifice of American prosperity crumbled into the ruins of depression. America was in pain and the Democrats had their first real issue in more than a generation. By 1932, unemployment stood at 24 percent—twenty-five million Americans were without a source of income. In the first four years of the Depression the value of stocks on the New York Exchange nosedived from $87 billion to $19 billion; farm prices dropped by 60 percent; wholesale prices fell by 38 percent, and real income was sliced in half. The Depression was that final, cataclysmic issue which precipitated the realigning election of 1932.

Radio was the weapon both sides used in the 1932 showdown. The contrast was vivid. "To the average radio fan, after a hard day's work, the thud-thud-thud of an average Hoover speech sounded like someone reading from a dictionary. . . . He could not get it through his head that there were people at the other end of those contraptions and connections."[16]

Roosevelt was a master of broadcasting. His natural talent for touching listeners was formidable, but was even more impressive when compared to Hoover's. FDR's Secretary of Labor Frances Perkins described Roosevelt delivering a radio address:

He did not and could not know them [the listeners] all individually, but he thought of them individually. He thought of them in family groups. He thought of them sitting around on a suburban porch after supper on a summer evening. He thought of them gathered around a dinner table at a family meal. He never thought of them as "the masses". . . . His voice and his facial expression as he spoke were those of an intimate friend. . . . As he talked his head would nod and his hands would move in simple, natural, comfortable gestures. His face would smile and light up as though he were actually sitting on the front porch or in the parlor with them. People felt this, and it bound them to him in affection. [17]

Roosevelt's skill at creating rapport over the radio was almost uncanny. In his second Fireside Chat, in July 1933, listeners heard the president stop his talk, ask for a glass of water, then heard the water being poured and sipped. FDR explained to the nation, "My friends, it's very hot here in Washington tonight." A radio address following the bank closings seemed to soothe the country's fears almost overnight, according to newspaper reports. Roosevelt was keenly aware of his radio rapport. "I know what I'll do when I retire," the president said. "I'll be one of those high-powered commentators."

The question must be asked again. Did the new means of communication contribute to the realignment of American politics? Just as during the periods before 1860 and 1896, the elements of realignment were all in place when America voted in 1932. As in the two previous realigning elections, there had been recent technological breakthroughs which had changed mass communications. Without a doubt, radio was the catalyst of political change. Whether such a statement could have been made if Roosevelt had not possessed not the radio persona he had, is not clear. From a media perspective, he was the right man at precisely the right time in history. Roosevelt understood the medium of radio as few of his political adversaries did.

The results of the Roosevelt realignment are written in the election returns and the voter registration forms. In the eight years from 1928 to 1936, the Democratic presidential vote increased from 15 to 27.8 million, and the Republican vote fell from 21.4 to 16.7 million. [18] The Roosevelt coalition of labor, Southern Democrats, urban ethnics, blacks, working class WASPs, and intellectuals would endure for more than a generation—until the pendulum would swing again. And the cycle would come with another new technology destined to change politics—television.

Even if there were such a thing as a pure, sterile political laboratory, Watergate tainted the formula to such an extent that it appears impossible to know if 1968 were truly a realigning election. There is adequate evidence that on the presidential level, at least, the Republican party is currently entrenched.

If, in fact, 1968 was a realigning (or dealigning) election, then it was a realignment triggered by television. By 1968, television had been in the American home for almost a generation. Early on it had been incorporated into politics, but never on the scale and sophistication of the 1968 Nixon campaign. What America saw on its TV screens in 1968 was the culmination of at least sixteen years of trial and error by politicians and their TV advisors. By 1968, TV was not an innocuous little box, but an established and powerfully influential medium. It was the greatest invention to date to persuade, convince, and motivate.

The story of the 1968 election may well have begun forty-five years earlier, when Vladimir Zworykin patented the electronic camera tube, the iconoscope. In 1926, Englishman John Baird successfully transmitted the first image of the human face on a primitive device which would someday send the image of Archie Bunker into homes around the globe. The technology of TV advanced rapidly and in 1928 (four years before FDR's election) the Federal Radio Commission awarded an experimental license to RCA's W2XBS. That same year General Electric televised its first drama. By 1937, there were seventeen experimental stations in operation. Two years later at the New York World's Fair, Roosevelt became the first president to appear on television. Commercial television was inaugurated in 1941, with CBS, RCA, and DuMont broadcasting to a paltry audience of only five to ten thousand viewers. In April of 1942, commercial television was suspended because of World War II; it would be several years after the war before television would explode as radio had a generation before.

The groups that coalesced around Franklin Roosevelt gave the Democrats a sustained hold on the White House for all but eight years between 1933 and 1969. One would have to go way back to the pre-Civil War period to find a time when the Democrats rode as high. Except when the magical FDR was a candidate, elections held during this period were—with few exceptions—rather competitive. Although it held the loyalties of a minority of the voters, the GOP did not wither and fade. Only once—in 1964—did the Republicans nominate a candidate who was slaughtered at the polls. The candidate, Barry Goldwater, was viewed by many as a conservative extremist. Looking at postwar politics, it is quite apparent that the two major parties were in relative balance, even though the Democrats remained the majority party.

The post-war period well into the 1960s was quite parallel to the years preceding the realigning elections of 1860, 1896, and 1932. Until the social fabric of the nation began to unravel, the country experienced a period of low inflation, high employment, social cohesion, and, above all, relative tranquility. It can be argued, of course, that there was nothing especially soothing about the postwar confrontations in Greece, Turkey, and Berlin. Nor was there anything pleasant about the Korean conflict, Suez War, or Cuban Missile Crisis. Yet people who look back at the twenty years between 1946 and 1966 often speak nostalgically. To much of the nation, those were the golden years, a time of national consolidation after the bitterness of Depression and the agony of war. It was an era when America got down to the business of making money and making babies, when all the world seemed to be crying out for Coca-Cola, IBM typewriters, and rock 'n' roll. American prestige was high. It was easy to feel good about America then. Every year brought newer, more wonderful consumer goods—large, eight-cylinder cars, dishwashers, televisions, air conditioners, electric lawn mowers, and more. The destiny of America appeared to be symbolized by the populating of suburbia, when new subdivisions, shopping centers, and highways gobbled up land at an incredible rate. *Excelsior*—America was growing ever larger, ever bigger, ever more powerful. No one could see around the corner of history back in the late 1940s, 1950s, and early 1960s. The political cycle was in its stable period then.

There was no abrupt end to the postwar dream world. Some historians date the beginnings of the madness to the Kennedy assassination in November 1963. In some places the golden age lingered a bit. By 1966, 1967, and 1968 there was no doubt that much of America was cannibalizing itself. There was no external enemy, unless one considered pajama-clad Vietnamese half a world away. No, the enemy was within—within the cities, the schools, the government, the bedrooms, ourselves. Perhaps it is too close to that period to make a fair judgment, but it seems that history will look back and say America as a whole went somewhat berserk during this period.

A war few wanted and still fewer understood bled the nation and divided the country as no issue had since the Civil War. Cities from coast to coast erupted in a orgy of violence, flame, and hatred. College students ripped apart their own campuses, closed them down, and took them over. National guardsmen killed unarmed students on a midwestern campus. Some young Americans were savagely beaten by police on the streets of Chicago. The word *revolution* applied to everything: the black revolution, the student revolution, the sexual revolution, the cultural revolution. A half million gathered at Woodstock to celebrate the dawn of a new age, while others retreated into communes, cults, and drugs. It was a time when the assassin struck at Robert Kennedy, Martin Luther King, and George Wallace. Parents were pitted against their children and their children lashed out against what they called the Establishment. For the most part the late 1960s were frenzied, tormented, ugly and utterly beyond comprehension, a period that made the previous twenty years seem utopian by comparison.

To the political scientist this period can easily be viewed as a cataclysmic event similar to the crises which led to the preceding cyclical realignments. Truly, what the nation experienced beginning in the mid-1960s was little short of a social civil war. By the time 1968 rolled around, the major parties would be challenged by outsiders—just as they had at other critical junctures in American history. Alabama Governor George Wallace launched an independent presidential campaign in reaction to the social convulsions sweeping the nation. Sen. Eugene McCarthy ran an insurgent's race within the Democratic party and ultimately forced incumbent Lyndon Johnson to withdraw.

While the national nightmare was going on, Richard Nixon was plotting his comeback from the depths of political obscurity. After a near miss in 1960, Nixon lost a race for the California governorship in 1962, and appeared destined for the political graveyard. What made the Nixon resurrection all the more amazing is that he was never perceived as a likable chap. But Nixon and his associates were aware of something the nation was not, that this was the television age and the medium could be totally controlled and controlling. When Nixon faced the decision of whether to run in 1968, this much was evident: "Television was the only answer, despite its sins against him in the past. But not just any kind of television. An uncommitted camera could do irreparable harm. His television would have to be controlled."[19] The Nixon campaign was to be the campaign of the television age—the perfect union of television and advertising. Television would take a political relic, a has-been who was scorned by many, and make him president. Approve of Nixon or not, it was television's finest moment in politics; the medium accomplished what was thought to be impossible.

By 1968, television was no stranger to presidential politics, and neither was political advertising on TV. Nixon's famous Checkers speech in September 1952, in which he invoked his wife's "good Republican cloth coat" and his daughter's cocker spaniel to save his place as vice-president on the Eisenhower ticket, was stunningly successful. Sixty million saw or heard the speech and Nixon received five million letters and telegrams. Nixon's running mate, the telegenic Dwight Eisenhower, who probably could have gotten by with only his smile and his war record, relied heavily on Madison Avenue. The general had twenty sixty-second commericals called "Eisenhower Answers the Nation." The ads were essentially question and answer sessions with so-called average citizens. Eisenhower's opponent, Adlai Stevenson, rejected such tactics, saying he didn't want to be sold like breakfast food.

In 1960, Nixon was overmatched by Kennedy's use of TV. Nixon had not yet learned how to control the medium. In fact, until October 25, 1960, Nixon never once appeared on national TV when he was in command of the circumstances.[20]

While Kennedy had the right ideas in 1960, Nixon would perfect them eight years later. "Kennedy realized that his most urgent campaign task was to become known for something other than his religion . . . the answer was television."[21] Kennedy obtained surveys showing that twice as many Americans counted on TV as their source of news as on any other medium. Kennedy never knowingly missed an opportunity for TV coverage. Campaign appearances were scheduled early in the day, allowing for film processing and editing and a guaranteed spot on the evening news. "Television played a unique and unprecedented role in the 1960 election with the first national debates between major party candidates aired to the entire viewing nation during the fall general election campaign."[22]

The supreme moment for the Massachusetts senator came in the televised debates with Nixon. One hundred and twenty million people saw all or part of the four debates. Much has been made of Nixon's beard, the pale, drawn expression, the evident pain from a knee injury. "A glimpse of Nixon showed him haggard; the lines on his face seemed like gashes and gave a fearful look."[23] By contrast, Kennedy was rested, suntanned, alert, and talked directly to the television audience and not his opponent. "What television audiences noted chiefly was the air of confidence, the nimbleness of mind that exuded from the young Kennedy."[24] It was said that during the 1960 campaign Kennedy's vitality virtually "crackled from the television tube."

Four years later, then incumbent Lyndon Johnson used television ads to what many believed was unfortunate excess. There was the "Daisy" ad, which was seen by fifty million viewers on September 7, 1964, and never seen again. In an effort to paint Barry Goldwater as a warmonger, the advertising firm of Doyle, Dane, and Bernbach created a highly controversial commercial. It showed a little girl picking a daisy and then dissolving into a cloud of atomic dust. Then there was the

Johnson ad showing two profiles of Goldwater. Called the two-faced Goldwater ad, the announcer challenged the viewer to pin Goldwater supporters down on their candidate's stance on the issues where he had made apparently contradictory statements. There was also a spot depicting a little girl eating an ice cream cone. The announcer stated that Goldwater voted against the nuclear test ban treaty and the assumption was if the Republican won, there would be nuclear testing once more. The viewer then heard the clicking sound of a geiger counter.

Nixon learned much from 1968. He had learned that television was not a neutral medium, nor was it an evil beast. It could be shaped and molded like a piece of moist clay. Nixon would draw upon the lessons of past campaigns, hire the best brains in TV and advertising and make himself president in spite of everything. Nixon's advisors put the candidate's image problem in plain language. Nixon was the guy who comes off as boring, dull, who was forty-two the day he was born. He was the kid who got a briefcase for Christmas and loved it, while other kids got footballs. "He looks like sombody hung him in a closet overnight and he jumps out in the morning with his suit all bunched up and starts saying 'I want to be president.' "[25] The challenge was to present Nixon as "the calm, warm, human pacifier." This would be a new Nixon, a mellow Nixon, a Nixon who could "bring us together."

Nixon and his aides set about rewriting generations of political wisdom. They all but ignored the print media, figuring that the newspaper reporters were enemies anyway. Also to be avoided were campaign appearances where Nixon would be confronted or have to respond spontaneously. There would be no debates, no "Meet the Press" or other interview shows. Nixon would avoid the inner cities and the college campuses like the plague in an attempt to shield himself from possible conflict. There would be public speeches, press releases, and television. Nixon would become the test tube candidate. Straight from Madison Avenue to Pennsylvania Avenue, with no stops in between where his beard might show or his suit become rumpled. The campaign would be antiseptic, sterile—and absolutely phony.

The main vehicle for Nixon's sanitized TV campaign was the so-called panel show with supposedly average citizens. The people selected for the panels would throw medicine ball questions at Nixon and he would slam them out of the park. No skilled journalist would get near the candidate. "The casual audience could hardly realize that these hometown panel shows were put together with approximately the same degree of spontaneity permitted in the construction of a space satellite."   With the studio audience carefully screened, Nixon would receive applause and standing ovations. News reporters covering the campaign had to watch from TV monitors in another room.

The Nixon commericals were masterpieces in marketing. They showed a warm, steady, secure Nixon addressing himself in the vaguest of terms to the problems of war, poverty, and social disenchantment. It didn't matter what Nixon *said*. The 1968 Nixon campaign wasn't much for issues. In the words of his own advisors it was a campaign designed to convey impressions and images. It was totally choreographed and Nixon danced through the script to perfection.

Once again, the coincidence of major technological advancement in the media just preceding realigning elections is too apparent to ignore. Lincoln's election in 1860 came after technology helped create the first mass circulation newspapers. The McKinley victory was achieved in the wake of technological change which built the exceptionally powerful daily press of the 1890s. Roosevelt's triumph in 1932 was aided greatly by the use of still another new technology, radio. And Nixon's vindication in 1968 was in large measure made possible only after he learned to control the new leviathan—television.

Throughout the nineteenth and twentieth centuries communications became increasingly pervasive and more personal. As it once had been hard to avoid the newsboy shouting "Extra, Extra," it became harder still to block out the sound of radio and impossible to silence TV. The mass media meant what they said. The masses were exposed to political messages and politicians as never before in history. By the early 1960s, there was no escaping the tube. Viewers had the option of watching the State of the Union address or primary election returns or not watching TV at all. Television—omnipresent and universal—controlled the American political scene.

In the political sphere, the continuing legacy of TV can be seen in the national political parties—what is left of them. Parties, the bridge between society and the state, began to crumble in front of the television leviathan. A pressure group is not affected by TV as is a party. Such a group is nothing more than an association of like-minded individuals who seek to influence policy. But for a party, its raison d'être is purely political. It was obvious by the mid-1960s that the party politician was no longer in charge of the medium; the party politician was being devoured by the TV monster he once thought was his ally. To those who still believed in parties, it was all new and terribly frightening.

Those looking for a harbinger of the new political era might well study Jimmy Carter's 1976 presidential campaign. In a political advertisement Carter said:

I started my own campaign twenty-one months ago. I didn't have any political organization. Not much money. Nobody knew who I was. We began to go from one living room to another; one labor hall to another . . . beauty parlors, restaurants . . . talking to people, and listening. To special interest groups I owe nothing. To the people I owe everything. [27]

Carter said nothing about pleading his case to big city bosses, suburban party chiefs, or national committeemen. Of course, Carter spoke to all of these. Yet by 1976, television had so radically changed American presidential campaigns that a major candidate did not have to prostrate himself before party honchos to win a nomination. When Carter talked of going into living rooms, he wasn't kidding. In his travels prior to the New York convention, Carter milked local television for all the exposure he could get. He was in the nation's living rooms night after night. Carter owed very little to the party hierarchy for making his name a household word and his candidacy credible. In an earlier time seeking the presidency without the blessing of party leaders would have been ludicrous; by Jimmy Carter's day, it made sense.

By the time Jimmy Carter began to transform himself from a Georgia governor of little distinction to the leader of the Free World, television had usurped much of the powers of the parties on the presidential level. Carter's theme was ideally suited for the tube. He wasn't selling partisanship. The message wasn't "vote for Jimmy Carter, Democrat." The pitch was, "a vote for Carter is a vote for trust, honesty, reliability, goodness, caring, responsiveness" and—for the first time in American political history—love. [28] The values Carter pushed might well have qualified him to be a local TV news anchorman. Carter was portrayed as a good guy in whom one could believe. There was little promotion of his skills as an administrator or his identity as a Democrat. For a medium where image far outshines substance, the Carter campaign was perfect for TV. Party allegiance was lost somewhere in the backwoods of the Carter campaign. It was necessary baggage, but not essential equipment.

The first cracks in the party colossus came when government and other institutions absorbed the traditional functions of party. The old foundation of patronage was replaced by the merit system. The need for a simple means of voter identification was lost when the public became wholly literate through public education. The party handout was unnecessary once government got into the social welfare business. The political boss who provided coal to warm frigid winter nights, a Christmas basket to feed the hungry, and a job referral service couldn't match government filling the same human needs.

By the post-New Deal era, parties were stripped of most of their day-to-day contact with the people. The parties retrenched and fell back on their original function—to make order out of the electoral system. Parties would continue to organize issues and options, to recruit political leaders, organize minorities, to promote consensus and legitimacy, to moderate and compromise political conflict, to bridge the separation of powers and, most importantly, to select candidates.[29] By the end of World War II, the days when the political boss or county chairman was a quasi-government providing direct constituent service were virtually over. But the party retained a bit of its historic functions to keep it alive and vibrant.

When Jimmy Carter ran for president, only 63 percent of the electorate identified with either party! Even those who called themselves Democrats or Republicans were more than likely to split their tickets. In a nation which prided itself on its two-party system, more people said they were independents than Republicans.[30] Recent polls indicate that a plurality of the voters now consider themselves to be independents. How distant is the day when a majority will hold no loyalty to either party?

Statistics can go on forever and still move in the same direction. It is well documented that the powerful emotional draw parties had on the American voter began to fade as government slowly began to pick up many of the same human services parties provided during their glory days in the latter nineteenth and twentieth centuries. Up to the Eisenhower years, Democrats could still be counted upon to vote for Democrats and Republicans for Republicans. In the 1960s, however, the steady erosion of party loyalty turned into a massive rebellion of political independence.

Precious few voters from the 1960s on could be taken for granted. Straight-ticket voters were fast becoming like the bald eagle, an endangered species. The American voter was finding parties irrelevant. Old psychological ties to parties, many of which dated back generations, largely dissolved during the 1960s. "All measures lead to the same conclusion. There has been a long-term decline of party allegiance, and a dramatic drop-off over the last decade. A large segment of the electorate now describes itself as independent, and even a larger proportion is behaving independently, showing little regard for party in electoral choice."[31]

So pervasive is the breakdown in party loyalty that a mere 38 percent of Wisconsin voters in 1974 felt there should even be party labels on the ballot. A nineteenth-century American, even a 1950s voter, would find in such a statement political heresy. Ask any

American to pick five words to describe himself and party affiliation won't be on the list.[32]

What is even more intriguing is that the two major political parties survived the loss of their *human service* functions, which occurred in the wake of FDR's welfare state. The parties inability to cope with their failure to supply jobs, food, and fuel should have appeared statistically in the 1940s and 1950s. It did not. Remember that in the early 1950s, two-thirds of the electorate still voted a straight party ticket and 90 percent still identified with one of the two national parties. Amazingly adaptable and resilient, the parties retained the loyalty of their supporters while the underpinning was cut out from under them. The parties simply focused their energies on their *political* functions— functions which pre-dated the role of human service provider.

That adaptation only delayed the inevitable. The assault on the parties did not abate. The danger this time came from an exciting new mode of communication, the television. The tube took away most of the *political* function of parties and this time the Democrats and Republicans had nothing to fall back upon. Television sent the parties reeling into a tailspin.

Today, stripped of their human service and political functions, the parties are in sorry shape. Recovery is nowhere in sight and the future looks bleak. How did the seemingly innocent television set, which is usually content just to sell Coca-Cola and packaged cereal, become the Achilles heel of the political parties? Moreover, what is the prognosis as the nation heads toward yet another realigning election?

The television—even primitive one-way television—strikes at the heart of political parties because it is a direct connection between the candidate and voter.

> The communications function, whereby party leaders communicate with the rank and file, and the latter in turn send messages up to the party leadership, has historically been a great raison d'être for political parties in egalitarian systems; but this function has increasingly been assumed by other structures, notably those organized around mass media of communications.[33]

Traditionally, American politics is a three-tiered system, with the party serving as an intermediary between the voter and the politician.[34] The party not only picked candidates and selected issues, but provided money, expertise, bodies, and the political savvy to run a campaign. The public, speaking directly or through business, labor, ethnic, or social service groups, was able to communicate to the politician using the party as a conduit. Especially when television is combined with the public opinion poll, the historic role of the party is abolished. The candidate speaks to the voter and the voter talks back to the candidate, with only Mr. Gallup there to count the numbers. The candidate can raise his own money and hire professional consultants to handle campaign logistics, direct mail, press relations, advertising, and television. The party can be left out of the process altogether. The candidate must dutifully follow the dictates of the consultant and heed the counsel of his public opinion polls; the party no longer has such influence.

At least on the national level, the TV studio has long replaced the smoke-filled room as a place where power is divided and nominations are won and lost. TV, said *Time* magazine, "more than any other single factor has cut loose candidates from parties and allowed them to inject themselves directly into the constituent consciousness."[35] A candidate's TV persona counts far more than his contacts with the party's hierarchy. TV has even blurred the seemingly obvious distinction between winning and losing. In the 1972 New Hampshire presidential primary, Sen. Edmund Muskie's plurality of 47 percent was interpreted as a loss to Sen. George McGovern—an interpretation which doomed the candidacy of the Maine senator. Four years later in the Iowa Democratic party caucuses, "uncommitted" won 37 percent of the vote and a vote-hungry Jimmy Carter came in second with 28 percent. A network correspondent called the Georgian the "clear winner" and Carter was off winging into the New Hampshire primary where he parlayed Iowa into a New England win and quickly found himself on the covers of both major news weeklies.

The capstone of TV as the new Leviathan was undoubtedly the election of Ronald Reagan in 1980. What could be more obvious than the accession to the White House of a politician whose roots were in entertainment and television, not political clubhouses? Even by Nixon's standards, Reagan was the quintessential TV candidate. Reagan needed a camera lens far more than a party label.

The presidential elections of 1980 and 1984 brought further evidence that parties are rapidly becoming as obsolete as the slide rule. Viewers voted for the person over the party. Even Ronald Reagan's landslide victories did pathetically little for grassroots Republicanism.

Might this be not the *realignment* so long anticipated, but *dealignment*? It seems that political theorists were looking for horses, but found zebras. For so long everyone stood the realignment watch. Maybe everyone was looking for a political event which may never again occur.

For all the ballyhoo of Reagan's 1984 landslide, there was little indication that the incumbent's coattails extended beyond his vice-president. Democrats picked up two seats in the Senate and lost fourteen in the House of Representatives in 1984. Democrats continued to control the vast majority of governorships and state legislative houses. Certainly a true Republican realignment would include more than the presidency and a slim hold on the Senate?

Equally intriguing is the gradual loss of voter allegiance to both parties. In 1952, 47 percent of the electorate identified themselves as Democrats, 22 percent as Republicans, and 22 percent as Independents. Thirty-two years later, an ABC-*Washington Post* poll showed that 39 percent called themselves Democrats, 27 percent Republicans, and 34 percent Independents.[36]

Political scientists and historians have probed and picked at the 1968 election as a child unwilling to eat a serving of spinach. Was Watergate of true consequence to the pattern of political ascendancy? One can wrestle with the facts forever without satisfaction. The undisputed fact is that Democrats won only one presidential election between 1968 and 1984, but still managed to hold on to congressional and local offices. If indeed a realignment took place, it was not as obvious as preceding political change.

As the nation moves farther and farther from 1968, it appears that historians may have been using the wrong yardstick to measure contemporary American politics. The phrases "Democratic era" or "Republican era" or "Federalist era" were for a couple of centuries a perfect way for historians to pigeonhole a political period. But not anymore. Television blurred party labels. Politicians like Nixon or Reagan could use television to advance personal ambition; they could travel alone without the baggage of political party.

The advent of true video democracy—direct democracy—does not bode well for political parties. Historically, the foundation of the political party is on the most local level, the precinct captain. The great political institutions were built with a firm base of citizen participation.

Assume for the moment that much of local government in America is practiced over an interactive communications system. Yes, such a situation may be forty or fifty years in the future, but even though revolutions in communications take decades to impact politics, those impacts are, as has been shown, both considerable and inevitable. What does direct democracy do to the party system?

Locally, the only need for a party is to mobilize the public on broad-based issues coming before the electronic public assembly. That is a minor function indeed compared to the traditional role of nominating candidates for office, running campaigns, and setting the political agenda. Local political parties were formerly able to survive the era of television because television largely ignored community politics. The parties survived the demassification of the media during the age of one-way cable TV because political programming was viewed by only a fraction of the population. There is little to suggest that parties will fare so well in the interactive age. The new conduit for political action and dialogue will be the television and its companion, the computer—not political parties.

Without firm roots on the local level, parties may never recover on the state and national levels. Dealignment may be a permanent fact of American political life. All those historians who still sift through election returns looking for realignment may have guessed wrong. Neither 1968 nor 1984 was 1860, or 1896, or 1932. No party has emerged to dominate the political scene. The country may be more conservative, but it is not overwhelmingly Republican.

If dealignment is truly the child of the mass media called television, what is the offspring of the newest technology? True acceptance of video democracy is incompatible with political parties. Video democracy is direct democracy; direct democracy is nonpartisan government; nonpartisan government is nonparty government. Whenever people vote directly on issues, when they themselves become the legislative branch, virtually no need remains for parties. Of course, parties will continue to function on the state and national levels, but the public will no longer feel the intense loyalty toward party that it once did.

The statement that all technological change in communications changes politics is both verifiable and applicable. The great change will be the advent of direct democracy—video democracy. A lesser but nonetheless important side effect will be the continued decline of the political party.

Notes

1.   William N. Chambers and Walter D. Burnham, eds., *The American Party Systems* (New York: Oxford Univ. Press, 1967), 289.

2.   David S. Broder, *The Party's Over* (New York: Harper and Row, 1971), 189.

3.   Frank Luther Mott, *American Journalism: A History: 1690-1960* (New York: Macmillan, 1962), 223.

4.   Ibid., 233.

5.   Chambers and Burnham, *American Party Systems*, 13.

6.   Jeter Allen Isely, *Horace Greeley and the Republican Party 1853-1861* (Princeton, N.J.: Princeton Univ. Press, 1947), 33-34.

7.   James MacGregor Burns, *The Deadlock of Democracy* (Englewood Cliffs, N.J.: Prentice-Hall, 1963), 61.

8.   Ibid., 77.

9.   Carl N. Degler, *Out of Our Past* (New York: Harper and Row, 1970), 334.

10.   Chambers and Burnham, *American Party System*, 300.

11.   Mott, *American Journalism*, 546.

12.   Allan Nevins, *The Evening Post* (New York: Boni and Liveright, 1922), 503.

13.   Louis W. Koenig, *Bryan* (New York: G. P. Putnam's Sons, 1971), 243.

14.   James David Barber, *The Pulse of Politics* (New York: Norton Simon, 1980), 246.

15.   David Burner, "The Democratic Party: 1910-1932," in Arthur M. Schlesinger, Jr., ed., *History of U. S. Political Parties Volume III* (New York, Chelsea House, 1973), 1828.

16.   Barber, *The Pulse of Politics*, 240.

17.   Ibid., 247.

18.   James L. Sundquist, "The Realignment of the 1930s," in James I. Lengle and Byron E. Shafer, eds., *Presidential Politics* (New York: St. Martin's, 1980), 398.

19.   Joe McGinnis, *The Selling of the President 1968* (New York: Trident Press, 1969), 34.

20.   Robert Spero, *The Duping of the American Voter* (New York: Lippincott & Crowell, 1980), 41.

21.   Ibid., 39.

22. John T. Willis, *Presidential Elections in Maryland* (Mt. Airy, MD: Lomond Publications, Inc., 1984), 121.

23. Erik Barnouw, *Tube of Plenty* (New York: Oxford Univ. Press, 1975), 274.

24. Ibid., 273.

25. Roger Ailes, in Barber, *The Pulse of Politics*, 300.

26. Ibid., 299.

27. Jimmy Carter, in Robert Spero, *The Duping of the American Voter*, 11.

28. Ibid., 139.

29. Chambers and Burnham, *American Party System*, 50.

30. Adam Clymer, "Studies Find Future in Political Parties," *The New York Times*, April 20, 1981, B6.

31. Ladd and Hadley, *Transformations*, 329.

32. Lance Morrow, "The Decline of Parties," *Time* 112, no. 21 (November 20, 1978): 42.

33. Everett Carl Ladd, Jr. and Charles D. Hadley, *Transformations of the American Party System* (New York: W. W. Norton & Co., 1975), 27.

34. Arthur M. Schlesinger, Jr., "The Crisis of the Two-Party System," *Current*, no. 214 (July/August 1979): 42.

35. Morrow, "The Decline of Parties," 42.

36. Morton Kondracke, "The Big Swing," *The New Republic*, (October 22, 1984): 13.

7

POLITICS AND
ONE-WAY CABLE

BEFORE MAKING THAT great leap into the age of interactive TV, let's ignore for a moment the networks and mass television and envision politics and television in an intermediate era—for many, an era already at hand. This is the age when TV has been demassified. Not mass media—but hundreds of little media. What will the age of one-way cable do to the political process? Will the dealignment of political parties continue as it did in the age of network dominance? What of political participation? Will voters remain passive observers as they did during the network era?

On the surface, the old, faithful TV set seemed to give each person a stake in the political process. That was illusionary, because the mere fact that politics was on the tube did not force the viewer to *feel* a part of the system. Quite the contrary, the public began to blur politics on the tube with television's primary responsibilities, which are to sell and to entertain. Politics became something to be observed as an aside, not something to be lived and experienced.

As television proved to be a disease for the political party, so it was for the body politic. Dealignment is a symptom of something gnawing at the spirit of democracy. Television brought politics into the home, but not the heart. As it came closer into view, politics became a more distant part of the daily lives of the American electorate. By the mid-1980s, politics and public affairs became just another TV show. It seemed no one would get especially upset if the primaries were cancelled after an unsuccessful season in the Nielsen ratings.

Cable TV offered no real or permanent solution to the disease of apathy tearing at the nation's political soul. Standard, one-way cable TV simply gave people an opportunity to tune out, watch the all-weather channel rather than a political debate, or a rugby match from Britain rather than the news. One has to wonder how much tuning out there will be once the entire nation is wired for cable or has access to alternative programming over the dish.

What cable has *not* done is in any way increase political participation or awareness. It may be accomplishing just the opposite by giving people a chance to avoid the network's force-feeding of politics.

As will be discussed later, true interactive cable has political implications far exceeding its older sister, one-way cable.

Television has given the public a sense of belonging, a certain visual intimacy with the electoral process. After all, the average American spends nine years of his lifetime in front of the tube.[1] One doesn't live with someone, or something, for that long without making it part of the family. TV coverage of presidential primaries is a perfect example. Regardless of the politics, primaries are great theater, a traveling road show where the banter of the network anchors is of greater interest than the campaign promises of candidates. The coverage brings millions upon millions of dollars of economic gain to the states holding presidential primaries. Small wonder that the number of presidential preference primaries has increased from sixteen states and the District of Columbia in 1968, to all but a handful of states today. People want to participate in televised sport, and presidential primaries are televised sport. "Television has given the ordinary citizen a new sense of entitlement in the political process."[2] Without belaboring the point, it should be clear by now that the increased use of primaries further diminishes the power of political parties. There is no smoke-filled room on prime time.

Exposure to politics on television must not be confused with genuine interest in politics. Yes, statistics show that 89 percent of the population gets its politics from the tube. While that statistic helps to explain the severing of the historic link between party and voter, it has not heightened public concern or participation. In the nation's bicentennial year, only 53 percent of the eligible voters went to the polls in the general election and a scant 28 percent bothered to vote in the primaries. In the national election two years later, the turnout was 34 percent. The unhappy fact is that 42 percent of all potential voters do not care enough about the outcome of elections.[3] One scholar predicts that the number of eligible voters will fall to 27 percent within a decade.[4] The cynic might say that the public has reacted to television politics much like the football fan has—over-exposure leads to boredom.

A discernible pattern emerges. Intense exposure of politics on television leads to a breakdown in party function, a loosening of attachments to political parties, and a rapid decline in citizen participation in politics. The most frequently used remedy for the growing problems facing the political system has been more democracy, generally in the form of more primaries and easier registration. The remedy has contributed to a worsening of the condition of the patient, since the more primaries there are, the lower the interest in them. The intent of reformers who embraced the primary was to increase participation. That goal has not been realized.[5]

Human nature, it seems, has been turned upside down. The more politics is brought to the people through mass media and direct primaries, the more people reject politics. In contemporary America the average citizen has the best opportunity in all of history to participate in the selection of leaders. What does the average citizen do? He stays home and allows his neighbor to vote. Usually his neighbor stays home, too.

Declining voter participation in light of increased TV coverage of politics can be explained by research. TV news does not reach the low interest voter, even though he may be watching. "It is well documented that when viewers watch Archie Bunker or Columbo, they are not deeply involved. And network news, because it contends with the dinner hour clamor, seems to receive even lower levels of attention than typical entertainment programming."[6] A study of TV campaign coverage showed that the typical issue is mentioned every third week for twenty seconds, and that most coverage focused on trivial campaign hoopla.[7] The most damning statistic of all concerning voter apathy was a panel survey of voters who watched and did not watch network news during the 1972 campaign. The panelists were graded on their awareness of eighteen campaign issues. The conclusion was that network news had absolutely no influence on what less interested voters learned about issues. Awareness was the same for those who did and did not watch TV news.[8]

It is well accepted that political participation is largely habit. If one's parents conscientiously went to the polls, the likelihood is that their children will follow when they become eligible to vote. And a habit lost is a habit hard to regain. That is why the present trend of declining voter participation is so distressing. The hundreds of hours each year of news and public affairs on network TV have done nothing to increase voter participation. If anything, the networks' coverage of politics has cracked the foundation of party politics and further weakened the system.

By the mid-1980s, politics was on its way to becoming a spectator sport, much like anything else on television. Research using an electroencephalograph attached to viewers' heads shows that their brains are dominated by alpha waves, the electrical waves predominant when the brain is relaxed, passive, unfocused, and basically not paying attention.[9] Is that the sort of vigorous citizen activism the Founding Fathers had in mind?

Where does the nation stand in the mid-1980s?

—Network TV is the dominant vehicle for disseminating political information.

—Political parties have seen many of their functions usurped by TV. The nation is in a process of apparent dealignment, with neither party able to hold the loyalty of the majority.

—Political participation is at a low ebb with no immediate prospect of rejuvenation.

All this is a consequence of TV's role as a homogenizing medium. What will occur, then, when TV is transformed into a more personal medium? When the viewer has access to hundreds of options across the cable or satellite dish? When the medium is demassified, will the present trends continue?

Television will continue to be the major source of political information. Reading is not likely to make a comeback. The future difference from our present era of network dominance is that people who do not want to be informed will no longer be forced to watch nationally televised public affairs as they have been under the network-controlled system. There will no longer be a single *viewing public*, but many *publics*. They will break down into groups of like-minded interest. Only a fraction of viewers will choose to watch news and public affairs shows when given scores of TV options every hour. A glimpse of the future can be seen in one study, an extensive, four-year examination of the demographics of TV viewing, completed a couple of years ago. During the research, 2,476 individuals were interviewed for ninety minutes each. The interviewees gave detailed descriptions of their viewing habits and degree of interest in 139 leisure activities. The groups were also broken down by education, income, sex, and geographic distribution. The overall conclusion was that the national TV audience was not nearly so homogeneous as product marketing people might have believed. In all, fourteen distinct viewing groups were identified.[10]

For example, the study dubbed the one group "mechanics and outdoor life" group, named after their leisure activities. Comprising the largest number of adults, this group was characterized in the study as being made up of blue-collar workers with an average age of twenty-nine. These viewers are interested in noncompetitive activities with an emphasis on physical accomplishment, such as fishing, camping, and auto repair. The survey says that this group has a strong need to create accomplishment and escape through shows high in adventure, drama, and suspense. Shows these viewers regularly tuned into include "The Six Million Dollar Man," "CHiPS," "Charlie's Angels," and "The Rockford Files." These viewers hold little interest in soap operas, game shows, theater, music, competitive sports, or news.[11] There is simply no way the members of the "mechanics and outdoor life" group would regularly watch cable public affairs broadcasting.

Another group that was differentiated in the study is "home and community centered." Demographically, this segment averages age forty-four, is female, married, and tends to be home during the day, cut off from adult contact. These viewers have, according to the authors, low aspirations and low creativity. As a group, the "home and community centered" people are partial to soap operas, talk shows, game shows, and TV religion.[12]   Cable-televised public affairs programming would not appeal to this group.

Yet a third group is seen by the researchers as "detached." They are men and women, often minorities, living in central cities, having the lowest income among the various groups, and possessing only a grade-school education. They have few interests or psychological needs, save for escape from boredom and a desire for status enhancement. They tend to watch movies, science fiction, soap operas, and crime series, all of which are seen as a means of escape.[13] These people are already nonparticipants in political life and it is very unlikely that cable-televised politics would interest them at all.

In fact, only three of the fourteen identifiable subgroups of viewers would be responsive to news and public affairs on the demassified tube. One of the three groups is heavily involved in arts and culture. This group is rather distinctive because of a high concentration of women, with an average age of forty-four and wide intellectual and cultural interests. This group is noted for its total lack of interest in household management. Sixty-nine percent of the group has some college education compared to thirty-three percent for the population as a whole. Group members seek to understand the world around them and are not looking for escape or enhanced status. They are among the most likely viewers of "Wall Street Week," "Sixty Minutes," "The MacNeil-Lehrer Report," and "Washington Week in Review." They are also nearly three times more likely to watch theater than the average viewer.[14] These people are conditioned to watching public television and would seemingly have no trouble finding the cable channel carrying public affairs. They obviously are highly motivated achievers with high interest in the world beyond the front door.

According to the study, one segment of news buffs is made up of men and women with an average age of forty-seven with a huge appetite for TV, especially information. These viewers are predominantly white collar and seek out information in order to make themselves more knowledgeable and socially interesting. Among the fourteen groups, the news buffs are first in frequency of viewing news commentary and second in the viewing of documentaries. The report does say that this group is not especially active in politics.[15] It is quite possible, however, that the new world of video may induce these people into becoming more involved in politics.

The third of the fourteen groups which may find itself inclined to watch political shows on cable is the one the authors call "cosmopolitan self enrichment." This is the most affluent of all the groups studied and also one of the best educated. It includes men and women with an average age of thirty-six. As a group they have diverse intellectual and cultural interests and have strong needs for intellectual stimulation and creative accomplishment. They are the heaviest users of the print medium and the lowest users of TV among all the demographic groups. "This is a segment of highly literate individuals who are selective in their exposure to all mass media and who are receptive only to material they believe to be informative and intellectually stimulating."[16]

As one can see by the study, the demassified medium simply allows these and other groups to watch what they are natually inclined to watch and ignore what they are natually inclined to ignore. The days when one had no choice but to watch the president's State of the Union message because all the networks carried it ends when the cable is installed.

If anything, the demassification of the media helps political parties regain some of the functions lost during the age of mass media.

On the national level, the familiar two-party system will exist as long as there is an electoral college. Since a presidential candidate must receive a *majority* of the electoral vote, there is a natural bias toward the retention of the two-party system. While many assert that the electoral college is inherently undemocratic because an individual vote from a large state is weighted far more heavily than one from a small state, there is no denying that the electoral college encourages two-party democracy. In fact, since there is no mention of political parties in the Constitution, the electoral college is the single most important institutional obstacle to a multiparty system.

Other than on the presidential level, parties may begin to reassert themselves, although dealignment appears to be a fact of political life. With network television no longer dominant, parties will be called upon again to fill their traditional function of linking candidate and voter.

Major market television has traditionally all but ignored local campaigns for state legislatures and city and county councils. The world of the demassified media promises more of the same. Parties will continue to monopolize political organization on the lowest level of the ladder. In fact, the role of parties on this level is likely to increase. With viewers so fragmented—watching so many varied shows—it will be nearly impossible to reach the majority of voters by advertising on any single channel. Therefore, it appears that candidates running for local and state office will once again come to rely on the parties to promote and publicize their candidacies.

When political scientists as well as average observers think of parties, the image that arises is not the local party nominating a candidate for judge in the orphans' court. The image is the mammouth and powerful national party, the party of McKinley or FDR. The advent of television sorely depleted the powers of the national party because candidates could go it alone on the national level. Even when the media are demassified, there is no indication that the national parties can ever regain the extraordinary loyalty of voters that they once possessed.

It is possible to speculate on a scenario which could reverse the trend toward dealignment. An extreme national crisis for which a president who is closely identified with a political party is held to blame might give voters an incentive to coalesce around the opposition party. But the more likely scenario harks back to 1976. Even after Watergate, voters did not punish all Republican officeholders. A Democratic president was elected, but overall party allegiance was largely unaffected.

What of participation? The real question is, can it get any worse? It has been demonstrated that mere exposure of politics to the great masses of Americans did nothing to increase participation. Quite the contrary, exposure, coupled with party dealignment, has led to a depoliticization of America. Virtually all statistical data shows that Americans are less partisan and less political than at any time in the nation's history.

What does demassification do to participation? Those who really care about public affairs will have more germane programming to watch. Each community with cable will have locally originated public affairs shows. While these may not be slick, they will certainly reflect the political issues and values of the community. But the person who doesn't care and never did care about public affairs will finally be able to watch TV and avoid politics altogether.

Save for elections where there are great and compelling issues, participation will probably continue to decline. Having a hundred options on a TV set cannot, in itself, increase political participation. The day may be approaching when politics is something your neighbor does.

Compared with other "revolutions" in communications, the demassification of television is unlikely to have a profound impact on politics. The recent trends of dealignment and the declining participation of the electorate will not be profoundly affected by the new technology. All demassification does is break the network monopoly over news and public affairs. When the grip of network radio was broken after World War II, radio became a medium of multiple options for the listener. So it will be with television. Cable, the satellite dish, and other new technologies offer plain old television— different, perhaps, but mainly lots more of it.

The true revolution of television has not and will not arrive with one-way cable. If there is to be a revolution, it will come when the home television becomes truly interactive. Then all the assumptions about the impact of cable TV break down. Not only politics but also participation will enter an entirely new phase.

Video democracy requires an interactive system. Once the two-way cable or related technology is installed, then America has a true opportunity to reverse more than a generation of apathy. Politics can again be what those who dreamed about democracy had in mind. Civic affairs can be a part of everyday existence. Video democracy offers a new lease on life for a system noted more for lethargy than vigor, for staleness than for innovation.

Notes

1.   Dennis Meredith, "Future World of Television—Another 'Revolution' Coming," *Science Digest* 88, no. 3 (September 1980): 16.

2.   Arthur M. Schlesinger, Jr., "The Crisis of the Two-Party System," *Current*, no. 214 (July/August 1979): 43.

3.   Dennis S. Ippolito and Thomas G. Walker, *Political Parties, Interest Groups and Public Policy* (Englewood Cliffs, N.J.: Prentice-Hall, 1980), 99.

4.   Thomas Madron, "Political Parties in the 1980s," *The Futurist* 13, no. 6 (December 1979): 465.

5.   Frank J. Sorauf, *Party Politics in America* (Boston: Little, Brown & Co. 1968), 102.

6.   Thomas E. Patterson and Robert D. McClure, "Television and the Less Interested Voter," *The Annals of the American Academy of Political Science* 425 (May 1976): 94.

7.   Ibid., 93.

8.   Ibid., 91.

9.   Meredith, "Future World," 20.

10. Ronald E. Frank and Marshall G. Greenberg, "Zooming in on TV Audiences," *Psychology Today* 13, no. 5 (October 1979): 92-114.

11. Ibid., 95.

12. Ibid., 99.

13. Ibid., 102.

14. Ibid., 98.

15. Ibid., 102.

16. Ibid., 103.

VIDEO DEMOCRACY

FOR JOE CITIZEN it had been a hard day at the office. Every day had been tough since the secretaries were replaced by the master audio-typist computer. Those machines were supposed to revolutionize correspondence, but, like all those "state of the art" gadgets, there seemed to be more bugs than bytes in the system. In theory, at least, Joe was supposed to be able to dictate a report and the audio-secretary would "hear" his words and print out a grammatically perfect document within three minutes. Technology always looked better in the sales brochure, Joe thought.

Joe programmed his microwave dinner, sat down in front of the tube, and switched it on with his remote. Quickly he flipped through the video menu looking for the sports section of the televised local newspaper. "It's funny," Joe thought, "everyone calls it the 'paper' even though it hasn't been published on newsprint for years." Around the turn of the century the publishers had figured it was a lot cheaper to transmit the news and advertising across the cable than to print and physically distribute the same information. With a touch of nostalgia, Joe remembered how as a child he enjoyed the feel and smell of real newspaper, the one his father brought home from work back in the eighties. In an instant the baseball standings flashed on the screen. "Nothing's changed," Joe said to himself. "The Yankees are still stuck in last place." Over the next few minutes Joe sampled the sports sections of three out-of-town papers in an effort to see what other sports writers were saying of his team's winning streak.

Before dinner, Joe decided to take a quick look at what would be on the tube that evening. Again, he called up the menu. Under the "entertainment" subsection, Joe found several interesting listings: there were the usual "live" shows from Broadway, Las Vegas and London; a symphony, a ballet, and an opera; a strip show from one of New York's spicier topless bars; several "made-for-video" movies, and some video casino gambling. Joe considered watching the video gambling, but realized there wasn't quite enough money in his account to cover the evening's program. Joe depressed the button marked "self-improvement." There was an especially long list of activities on the tube ranging from isometric exercises for arthritis victims to a lesson called "the magic of pastas" by some Italian chef Joe had never heard of. He could spend the evening auditing a course on financial planning, but he had already missed the first three classes, so he decided against that.

Then Joe pressed the "public and civic affairs" button. The screen flashed a series of notices: "Public Works Open Forum, channel 7 B at 7:30; The Search for a New Superintendent, Channel 8 C at 8; Hospital Workers Ask for a Raise, channel 9 B at 8; Community Vandalism and the Police, channel 7 D at 8:30; A New Fire Station, channel 7 A at 9; a general Town Meeting, channel 8 B at 9:30."

The Public Works Open Forum piqued Joe's interest. Just this morning he had almost split an axle on a pothole while driving to work. He really wanted to tell those bureaucrats to get going filling those potholes. "What could be the delay?" he asked himself.

Joe lived in Mediaville, a community of 50,000 about thirty miles from the city. A decade before, the old town council chamber was converted to a TV studio. That occurred when the entire town had been wired for two-way cable. Each home had a computer which interacted with the cable TV system. For a long time after the town had the cable, it also kept the town council. Council meetings were televised and council members frequently asked residents to cast "votes" giving their opinions on local issues. Invariably, the council members voted exactly as the residents responded.

At one point, a bill passed the council allowing that the votes cast by the viewers be considered advisory. That seemed reasonable enough, since none of the council members had the independence to vote otherwise. A few years later, a referendum passed saying that the cable votes would be legally binding in certain situations, as long as the voter inserted the mag-strip card issued by the board of elections into the machine to verify that he was a registered voter. Such situations consisted of the approval of the annual town budget, changes in traffic patterns, and certain ceremonial issues—like presenting a certificate to famous visitors to town.

About that time the same idea seemed to strike everyone in town at once. Why *bother* to have a council at all? The members just collected salaries, took up office space, never showed a whole lot more sense than the guy sitting at home pushing buttons, and now, were serving only as mouthpieces for viewers anyway. Oh, the council members were pretty upset about the prospect of being cast aside like an obsolete piece of machinery. But eventually they got used to it. The mayor, now that was another story. He saw himself as a U.S. Senator someday, well at least a Congressman. He was not at all pleased when the voters told him to take his ambitions elsewhere. In his stead the voters hired a bright young woman who had a masters in public administration and had run another community's budget office. They called her city manager. No one knew if she was a Republican, a Democrat, or unaffiliated. The job of city manager was nonpartisan.

That does not mean that Mediaville as a whole was nonpartisan— far from it. Politics remained very intense, sometimes churning up bitter feelings. With no council to serve as a buffer on public issues, it was citizen against citizen. And that could get pretty touchy if folks on opposing sides of an issue were neighbors.

But people enjoyed their politics in Mediaville, far more so than before the council was abolished and the mayor was sent into political exile. On any given evening, up to a third of all voters would participate in one or more televised committee hearings. Subcommittee sessions were limited to certain people—who naturally participated while sitting at home, since the cable system was closed so that the company could narrowcast to a select group. On the big issues, it was common for 75 percent of the residents to vote.

Joe sat back collecting his thoughts about potholes. He was determined to convince his fellow citizens that they had not given potholes their due priority.

It was 7:30. Joe punched up channel 7 B. The meeting had begun. On the screen he saw the town's public works director, who was rambling on about the budget for snow removal and was asking for a supplemental appropriation to pay for overtime road crews when there is a snowstorm. The public works director motioned to a large pie-chart, which immediately popped up on the home screen. The discussion continued on the need for a more flexible budget in wintertime. When the public works director finally asked for viewer comments, Joe figured this would be as good a time as any to get his two cents in.

Joe punched the keyboard button marked "response." Then he typed the following statement: "The potholes in this town are horrendous. Today I drove the length of Main Street and counted fifteen potholes. Public Works committed itself to filling the holes and they haven't done a thing. Before we talk about supplemental money, let's deal with the potholes." Joe decided to sign his name to his statement, although he could have pushed the "anonymous" button. The public works director, seeing that someone had responded, typed something into his keyboard and within a couple of seconds all the viewers watching were able to read Joe's statement on their home screens.

Somewhat defensively the bureaucrat noted that his crews had filled more than one hundred potholes over the past five months, but the problem was just too big. He acknowledged that Main Street was not in the best condition.

Joe was not satisfied with that explanation. Again, he pushed the response button. He typed these words: "I make a motion that the public works department be required to fill all the potholes on Main Street within thirty days. Signed: Joe Citizen."

The public works director saw a green light flashing, indicating that someone had made a motion. Joe's motion was then flashed on the home screens. The public works director called for "seconds" to Joe's motion—under the rules of procedure, a motion needed the support of 20 percent of the people watching before it could come up for a full debate. All across Mediaville people sitting in living rooms, bedrooms, or wherever voted to second Joe's motion. The motion received 40 percent of the recorded votes and therefore merited discussion.

As moderator, the public works director called for opposing views. Joe, watching at home, would have to sit still and listen to the opposition before responding. When his turn to debate came, Joe would have two options. He could continue to type his responses into the terminal or, as the original sponsor of the motion, he could ask for the cable company's microwave truck to come to his house and allow him to argue his case visually. He punched the button indicating his opting for the latter. Fifteen minutes later a bright blue van with a yellow rod attached to a mast pulled up in front of Joe's house. Two technicians quickly established a microwave signal back to the cable studio (once called Town Hall). Then they brought a light, a camera, a tripod, and a microphone into Joe's living room. They placed the camera next to the TV so that Joe could observe and respond to what was being said on the tube during the pothole debate.

Opponents to Joe's motion were making their pitch. Mostly the objections came from people who never traveled on Main Street and from those who took the bus to work. Joe figured that any rational person who drives could never be against his motion. Someone asked how much it would cost to fill each pothole. The public works director said $50. Someone else inquired over the cable whether Main Street traffic would have to be detoured while potholes were being filled and the response was, "No, because potholes are filled one lane at a time." Another person asked if the town could be sued if the potholes were not filled and someone had an accident. The bureaucrat said he didn't know and opened the question up to any lawyers watching. Two responded, and the debate continued.

Finally, it was Joe's turn to speak. Although he had been on the cable countless times, Joe always felt a tinge of nervousness when the hot TV lights turned on. "I guess," he said to himself, "I don't want to seem like a fool in front of my friends. But sometimes they look pretty foolish themselves."

Joe cleared his throat and began to talk. Out of the corner of his eye he saw his face on the screen.

"I have been listening to all the arguments against filling the Main Street potholes," Joe said in a conversational voice. "A lot of them make sense. But let me say this. First, Public Works said a long time ago that they'd take care of the potholes. So far they haven't. Secondly, it is not all that much money. A single accident caused by someone hitting a pothole could cost the city much more than filling all the potholes on Main Street. Finally, Main Street is the heart of our community. It's our showcase. If we can't make Main Street look good, why bother promoting our town? Why let visitors come away from Mediaville seeing only our Main Street potholes?"

Joe suspected the last comment would score a lot of points, since most people in town were very image-conscious. The video debate volleyed on for another twenty minutes or so, which by local standards was pretty short. Often these debates lasted hours before a final vote was taken. When Mediaville first began video democracy, the debates took longer still. Everyone wanted to make his point on TV or as some of the townsfolk said, "Everyone wanted to be a star." But people were used to the system now. And just as had been the case with council members, everyone knew who the loudmouths were, those people who had to be heard on every issue regardless of how well informed they were. And everyone knew who the thoughtful citizens were, the ones who did their homework, studied the issues, and made sense when they spoke across the cable.

Finally, the debate ended. The public works director called for a vote—yes or no on Joe's motion. In a second the votes were tabulated and displayed on the screen: Yes, 1,567; No, 985. Main Street would be paved within a month. The public works director appointed Joe and two others to be an overseeing committee and report back to the community within a month on the progress of the street repairs. The director notified people who voted against the motion that it could still be appealed if they could circulate a video petition and bring it before the committee of video appeals within one week.

Joe sat back after the camera crew left his house and thought back to the days when video democracy first got started. He remembered the skeptics. It would never work, they said. A town needs *elected* leaders. Nothing will ever get done. No one will watch the thing. The system won't be credible. All the *wrong* people will vote. The town will be turned over to the contractors or the teachers or the labor unions or the businessmen or the senior citizens or the churches or the people on welfare. Nobody will speak for the guy in the street. There'll be chaos.

Well, there *was* confusion for a while, until the bugs were straightened out. As Joe knew, there were always bugs. The people didn't know whom to contact when they had a personal problem. Eventually, people realized they could get the town government to address problems simply by entering their grievances into the system; a computer automatically forwarded the complaint to the right government agency and then to the right bureaucrat. Soon people realized that the new system serviced constituents faster than the old method of calling council members and waiting for them to shake the bureaucracy.

Yes, there were times when one interest group dominated the system. Usually it was on fairly narrow issues. Joe recalled the time when a group of older people wanted a new senior citizens' center built. Their proposed plan was expensive, but boy, did they ever want that center. The campaign leaders got birth records from the health department and for days before the video debate they called everyone in the phone book over age fifty-five. Then each of those people got postcards telling them precisely when to watch the public affairs channels. It seemed to Joe that thousands of new voters participated in the video democracy the night that the senior center came to a vote. Joe voted with the seniors. It was against his economic interest, of course,—as he remembered it, the building fund raised his taxes several dollars—but he knew that the issue meant a great deal to the elderly and he saw its usefulness, so he went along with it.

There were times when the majority would dig in its heels. Joe reflected on the last contract with the town's public school teachers.

They wanted what he considered an outrageous wage increase. The subcommittee, which was composed of educators, lawyers, and parents, turned the teachers down, as did the entire Education Committee, but the teachers took the issue to the voters. The committee was aware that the teachers were organizing to bring out a big vote. Meetings were held. The two sides, the Education Committee and the teachers, were unable to compromise. So the committee publicized the time of the final vote. When the vote came, the teachers were no match for the well-organized majority. The majority prevailed.

Basically, the system worked, Joe said to himself. People got involved. They read, they studied and they participated. Common sense held extreme ideas in check. No one felt left out. Joe and his neighbors knew that any issue which is absolutely crucial to the survival of a group would never be turned down. The overall tranquility and cohesion of life in Mediaville was too important.

Joe thought about the Main Street potholes. He had succeeded in making the community look at the blight on Main Street. The street would soon be fixed, and Joe felt good about that. And good about living in Mediaville.

Is it fantasy? Today, yes; but not tomorrow—the technology already exists to make the video democracy of Mediaville a reality. What is suggested here goes far beyond video voting per se. Video voting is merely the movement of the ballot box into the home, creating a kind of electronic absentee ballot. There is nothing particularly radical about that. As discussed earlier, video voting will come when the handicapped, the elderly, those who must stay home with young children, and others unable to go to the polling places themselves realize that no longer should they have to.

The step beyond video voting holds many more ramifications and complexities, but offers far greater rewards. That step involves the implementation of true direct democracy. The Constitution is largely silent on local self-government. There are no legal barriers to stop most villages, towns, and small city governments from becoming direct democracies. Ordinarily small communities do not wrestle with complex questions involving weapons systems, changes in the income tax code, or environmental laws. Nor do local governments deal with significant moral issues (which are largely reserved for the states) such as the death penalty, euthanasia, and divorce laws. Local governments function in a nuts and bolts world of streets, sewers, schools, and public safety. Even the most complex local issues are within the intellectual grasp of most citizens. Elected officials with minimum expertise in these specialized areas have been voting on such issues for years. Common sense applied to local issues yields common sense solutions.

Video democracy offers the promise of better, more efficient local government. The people speak directly to the bureaucracy and the bureaucracy is responsible directly to the people without legislative intermediaries. In local government, the only true function of a legislative branch is deliberative—to examine policy alternatives and make decisions based on knowledge. There is no reason why an informed electorate of several thousand could not gather, digest, and discuss that same information and then make a reasoned choice among policy options.

Skeptics might say that a video democracy would be characterized by confusion and discord. Quite the opposite is true. The bureaucracy would be well aware that the people finally would have full legislative authority and therefore political legitimacy. And the people would know that they and they alone have the power to effect policy. Video democracy finally dispels the worn-out cliché often accurately applied to government: everyone gripes about politics but no one does anything about it. There will be no blaming the politicians when government fails to respond to problems. After all, there will no longer be such a thing as a professional politician. What is changing is not the *institution* of government, but its structure. The lines of communication and legislation may be different, but there remains a formal process.

In many respects, a video democracy strips away the charade of government. In the studies of Levittown, Eastport, and New Haven the people are either unconcerned about government or have convinced themselves that they have power, when, in fact, they are powerless. In the government of tomorrow there is no scapegoat. The citizen must look first to himself to see both the source of power and the cause of governmental failure.

All that is sacrificed is a political apparatus which, people will find, was of minimal value anyway. When people have an opportunity to run their own government and deal with issues directly, there is no need for a whole class of intermediaries, the professional politicians. A council is an expensive luxury for local government. No doubt it is a necessity today, but given the technological tools, it could become utterly superfluous. Council members draw salaries, have clerks and secretaries, take up office space, and can spend only a small portion of their time and energies on their governmental duties, since most small-town councils are part-time affairs anyway.

Let there be a nonpartisan administrative executive, much like a school system superintendent. But the local politicians whose membership on a city council sometimes may not be motivated solely by public-spiritedness become utterly useless in the video age. The average citizen could easily develop equal governmental expertise and begin to function in their stead.

Moreover, the new video democracy lessens the likelihood for political corruption—the bane of political legitimacy. Corruption eats at the soul of local government. Who is left to bribe when legislative power is so equally and widely dispersed? Faith in government can be restored when the public can be assured that there is no political caste benefiting directly or indirectly from positions of power. The power brokers, who once were able to touch a couple of council members and effect policy, now must deal with public opinion. Logic and fact will carry far more weight than how much a particular lobbyist will contribute in the next campaign for council seats.

Applying direct democracy to federal and state governments is unwise and unworkable. First, sheer numbers of participants would make the system far too unwieldly. Second, the more complex issues require full-time legislative and executive attention. Third, and perhaps more to the point, we would have to scrap the Federal and State Constitutions. But video democracy could work both efficiently and effectively on a local level as long as no one attempts to graft the new system on to the old. As has been pointed out already, direct democracy works so long as it is not filtered through an indirect system. It is an either/or situation, but not both. Trying to run a government with people voting at home to inform their legislators what to do is like trying to hit a baseball with a hockey stick—it's the wrong tool.

As in Mediaville, the local government wishing to try direct democracy must first abolish itself. The People become both legislature and executive. The bureaucracy stays in place as does a nonpartisan community administration. A committee system would be a fine method to manage the work load and bring expertise and special knowledge to those issues requiring such. The community could also hire consultants. But the legal power of government would reside in the electronic town meeting—much like the often-celebrated New England town meeting. All authority would flow from the meeting and all responsibility flow to it. The concept is utterly practical and eminently democratic.

The most often-heard criticism of direct democracy is that special interests would control the system. Not so. Under a representative government a special interest group only has to influence a majority of the council members, by ethical or unethical means. In a direct democracy, the same group would have to make a reasoned, logical argument before the entire community to win approval. Would minority rights be trampled? With adequate institutional protections, there is nothing to indicate that a direct democracy would be any more threatening to minority rights than an indirect system. Since a direct democracy would have to be adopted only by comparatively small communities, most everyone would be aware of the most sensitive issues involving minorities.

Essentially, the same variety of safeguards used to protect minority interests in a representative system can be adapted to direct democracy. On various public issues a two-thirds or even three-quarters majority could be required; the more fundamental the issue the greater the vote needed to pass the measure. An entire series of committees and boards of appeal could be constructed. Like the court system, the rights of the group and individual would be assured because of the many gatekeepers—no one vote by the entire community would be final or fatal to a minority's vital interest. The computer democracy could be set up allowing for the tallying of votes in geographic districts. Again, legislation would have to be approved by a cross-section of voters. Clearly, rules could be devised which would make it impossible for video voters in one section of the community to gang up on one another. It would even be possible (though perhaps not Constitutional) to make certain that legislation receive wide support from various or all demographic groups. The computer could be programmed to tabulate votes along racial, religious, age, income, geographic, and educational subgroups. In theory, a bill would need at least 30 percent support from each of the subgroups in order to become law.

Finally, the CONSENSOR experiment shows that intensity can be factored into a voting system. A very high intensity reading from a minority group against a particular piece of legislation could be considered a veto. Or, in theory, if any group voted 90 percent or more against a bill, that would be a veto.

A direct video democracy can protect minority rights as well as an indirect democracy. The worst fears of Madison, de Tocqueville, and Bryce do not have to be realized.

There is no stone tablet saying that local government must be a partisan affair. Indeed, many communities, large and small, have long abandoned political partisanship in favor of non-partisan council elections. These communities continue to have responsible, honest government despite the fact that there are no Republicans and no

Democrats. There is no reason why the same principle of nonpartisanship could not be applied to direct democracy. There is no need for party because there is no one to nominate and no election for office. In a direct democracy votes are on *issues*, not individuals. The only time a person would face the electorate would be if he is being considered for such positions as police chief, school superintendent, or the like.

The bottom line question in a direct democracy concerns participation. Obviously, government cannot be effectively run by a small cadre of dedicated activists. It demands mass popular support. In many communities citizen participation in public affairs is an embarrassment. School boards, councils and various public commissions often play to empty houses. Nationally, public interest in elections runs well behind the World Series, perhaps slightly ahead of the NBA championship.

The central point is that voter apathy and public noninvolvement cannot get much worse before the American system—on local, state, and national levels—is disgraced. One must assume that people do care and that they want to participate in decision making that affects their own lives. Government in America has not seriously reexamined itself since its beginnings. There have been reforms, but not deep reevaluations. The time and technology have arrived for American local government to come to grips with citizen nonparticipation. Today (if not literally today, literally tomorrow), local communities have the power finally to give government back to the people—to live the dream of Rousseau.

The central plea of this book is that local communities experiment with direct democracy. No doubt corporate and university sponsorship can be found to help implement true direct democracy. Try it. Try it for a limited period, say a year or two. Try it in a community which already has an interactive cable TV system. Simply make sure that each citizen has a terminal and that there are safeguards to identify and verify voters and voting.

Which communities should try direct democracy? Use Rousseau's model or the New England town meeting. The communities should be small enough that the problems are not too complex to be manageable, but large enough that a diversity of opinion can be expressed. Don't be afraid of conflict, because conflict becomes compromise when confronted by reason. Don't be afraid of the common man, because common men have been running the government from the beginning. Don't be afraid of change; self-rule can be the product of change.

If representative government has grown ineffective, stale, and boring, why not experiment? Direct democracy can work. As a system it can be sensitive to minority rights, responsive to challenging problems, and effective in balancing competing interests.

Why not be several steps ahead of technology? Once the hardware is installed, which is inevitable, Americans might stumble into some distorted form of direct democracy, a hybrid which will not work, some species of George Gallup Looks at Sewers—with a legislative body deciding whether to follow the polls. Why leave the development and implementation of direct democracy to chance? In science, planning always precedes the experiment. Why in political science should the experiment precede the planning? Let local governments intelligently set up experiments with direct democracy and adapt the technology to the experiment. There is no reason to wait until the technology is placed in the home before designing a system of direct democracy. There is nothing sacred about the representative system.

De Tocqueville was right in saying that one very special characteristic of democracies is that they are primarily reactive. Democracies tend to wait until a sore is infected before treating the wound. They exist on the crisis theory. Long ago, America allowed itself to be victimized by industrialization. Hardly a week goes by without a major news story about shipyard workers poisoned by asbestos, lakes deadened by acid rain, or products recalled because of a significant health risk. The daily threat of a nuclear war or accident is a painfully obvious reminder that the atomic genie slipped out of the bottle before man developed the institutions to control it.

It has been made clear here that the technology for a political revolution is sitting on our doorstep. In some places, like Columbus, Ohio, it has already entered the house. Like it or not, someday Americans will have to reconcile their system of government with the new technology. The technology of choice may not ultimately be cable TV—although the guess here is that cable is the most logical alternative. A haphazard, mindless adoption of the new interactive technology to politics and government courts disaster. A good plan is an antidote to eventual political crisis.

Why not have each state create a commission to study the impact of interactive cable on politics? If airlines, banks, and retail stores have devoted millions to studying the same technology, why shouldn't government do the same? A commission could comprise technical experts as well as politicians and the lay community, and would be asked to identify one or two towns or small cities in each state that would be asked to try video democracy for a limited period. All households in the community would be equipped with an interactive system; obviously, the community selected would already have a one-way cable system, which could be upgraded with the financial help of the communications industry. From its inception, cable has been viewed as a quasi-public utility, paying franchise fees to the community. It is entirely appropriate that the industry support a public function using its system. Stores, banks, airlines, and other business would also contribute to the wiring of the town, since they would benefit most directly from an interactive system.

The commission would oversee an experiment in direct democracy. It would set up basic ground rules concerning such details as the number of video town meetings to be held, the structure of committees, qualifications for voters, the selection of a nonpartisan town administrator, the process of appeal, and overall parliamentary procedure for video debate and voting.

The collective courage needed for a community to participate in such an experiment would be considerable. Such a step is no less than starting from scratch, the abolition of generations of government by elected representatives and habits and attitudes of voters. No one should doubt the enormous sacrifice the elected representatives would have to make to put themselves out of business even for a limited period.

Yet such an experiment is wholly consistent and true to the most basic American values. As a people, Americans love to tinker, invent, experiment. Why not apply the same creativity to politics and government as might be applied to building better mousetraps? The payoff can be as great as the failure to experiment can be disastrous. The plus side offers a historically unique opportunity to reverse years of declining voter participation. Video democracy offers a chance at a democratic renaissance in which the average person once again feels that government belongs to him.

Video democracy returns government to the people, quickly and efficiently. For the average voter most politicians quickly begin to become clones of each other. By definition and by evolution, the current system of elections breeds apathy and cynicism. A campaign promise broken once is a promise broken a thousand times. And a voter disillusioned once may be disillusioned forever. At long last technology has given American communities the opportunity to return to the purest form of democracy. It is a democracy thoroughly consistent with its past and totally in tune with its future. Those who remain apathetic and cynical when they have an opportunity to participate directly in local government are lost causes politically. But too many were lost along the way only because the system was mired in electoral politics.

What of state and federal governments? While not overtly changing the large, complex institutions of American government, video democracies would have a positive impact. Clearly, a citizen who must now inform himself on local issues would not close his mind to state, national, and international affairs. To be familiar with the police department budget, zoning policy, and landfills means that a voter is also likely to inquire about cruise missiles, the state income tax, and Central America. People who suddenly feel the responsibility and enjoyment of civic participation would logically become increasingly concerned with the world beyond their home town.

A video democracy also provides a mass training-ground for leaders. No longer will only a dozen council members receive experience in the operation of government—but thousands in each community. Several times a week people will view and participate in government. Some will be inspired to run for office.

As a people, Americans would become skilled at politics. Under a system of video democracy, citizens are asked to research and assimilate information and then debate the merits of various proposals and finally to compromise and reach a consensus. The acquisition of these skills makes a person a citizen in action and not merely in name. The entire governmental system cannot help but benefit from a more enlightened electorate.

Some might argue that these concepts view the public through rose-colored glasses, that the average person is either unable or disinclined to give much of himself to the affairs of local government. The fact is that Americans were once highly political. A hundred years ago Americans were much more likely to vote and to be actively involved in politics than they are now. Today, Americans remain political and civic-minded, but in another sense. We are a nation of joiners. Voluntarism is synonymous with contemporary America. We belong to PTAs, neighborhood groups, service organizations, religious social action groups, environmental organizations, issue groups and so forth. The list is endless. Never has there been such a plethora of organizations and people willing to devote time, energy, and money for the sake of a cause. All groups seek to change, improve, and convince. They are inherently political. Over the past century Americans have redirected their efforts away from partisan politics to nonpartisan organizations; they have invested in causes, not government. But all joiners are potential recruits for a video democracy. They are people looking for an outlet, a forum to express their opinions, a chance to listen and be heard. The potential citizen base exists. Once the technology is in place, the video citizen will appear in great numbers.

Ultimately, any governmental system is only as good as its people. The Platonic philosopher-king would be an ideal system of government, if one could be certain the leader would be the perfect philosopher-king. And so it is with democracy. It is the conviction here that deep down Americans want to participate, want to rule themselves. Given the opportunity, Americans would rule themselves with justice, compassion and, most of all, common sense.

Direct democracy deserves a chance.

One further issue which must be addressed falls under the heading of privacy. With the direct democracy experiment Americans must clearly understand precisely what is being invited into the home. The two-way cable (or related technology) is not harmless. Potentially, it is an Orwellian fantasy. To some civil libertarians the prospect of interactive TV in the house is nothing more than an electronic leash, a grave threat to privacy and civil liberties. "What we will be doing is striking a Faustian bargain, where the Devil offers us all these good things at the cost of our souls," writes MIT computer scientist Joseph Weizenbaum. "I'm sure it starts out benignly. Why worry about an anti-pilferage device? We don't pilfer. But clearly the opportunity is here for surveillance on a colossal scale. We may be cementing things into place, that if we thought about it, we may not want at all."[1] As Gustave M. Hauser, the president of Warner-Amex cable says, "People who buy the service will simply have to accept that they give up a bit of privacy for it."[2]

Defenders of the technology liken the computer to the telephone. No one is happy that calls are recorded, but the practice is taken for granted. The intrusion of the computer will become matter-of-fact.

Who will control the information? Will cable companies be able to sell socioeconomic data to advertisers wishing to target an audience? Will creditors have access to personal financial records? Will government be able to pick apart an individual's electronic files? And will the bookburners be able to purge the computers of material they feel is offensive?

Here's what one QUBE subscriber said about electronic snooping:

It's a little uncanny. They know exactly what you are watching. I like the ability to press a button and get what I want right in the house. But, of course, one gives away all sorts of opinions in the surveys—do you believe in premarital sex, capital punishment and all those things. One has to assume that they are not going to misuse that information. If I had reason to believe that trust had been violated, I'd obviously be very concerned and would certainly cancel the service. I would hope QUBE never causes me to be afraid to push buttons.[3]

Most Americans share a grave concern over the potential loss of privacy. A 1979 Louis Harris poll showed that 54 percent of those surveyed said computers were a threat to privacy and 63 percent agreed with the statement, if privacy is to be preserved, the use of computers must be sharply restricted in the future. The Harris study concluded that privacy should become one of the fundamental rights of a just society.[4]

Surveys such as the Harris poll speak of computers in the abstract. Those who have studied interactive TV find that subscribers are blissfully unaware of electronic eavesdropping. "The odd thing is that the privacy question is seldom raised by the subscribers themselves. It could be that the privacy issue is a slow time bomb awaiting detonation by some dramatic incident or cause célèbre, or that privacy is far less highly prized in our time than it was in the past."[5]

A minor political furor arose in Columbus when Mayor Tom Moody admitted that more than a couple of X-rated films had crossed the cable into his home. Moody defended his viewing habits by saying it was part of his job to see what the cable franchisers sent out on the cable. Everyone had a good chuckle at Moody's expense and that was that. The incident should have raised more than eyebrows. People *do* know what the mayor is watching in the privacy of his home. With a slightly more sophisticated keyboard than QUBE has, they'll know what he is reading, writing, and to some extent thinking. A scenario that has a political candidate defending his subscription to a radical journal he received across his TV and was billed for electronically is not far fetched. Imagine the uproar in a community if it was disclosed that the mayor occasionally called up *Pravda* from the video files of the university library. The possibilities are legion for intrusion into the personal lives of both public servants and private citizens. QUBE has been called "a system that can wreak havoc through the creation of shame and by manipulating the fear of shame. It can monitor the spending habits and cultural tastes of individuals within a family. In the hands of the unscrupulous it could bring misery and terror into peoples' lives."[6]

Sir Thomas More was beheaded for defending freedom of conscience. Does the loss of conscience begin with the loss of privacy? Can the monster be controlled? Americans have developed a healthy skepticism of technology when it comes to their *physical* health and safety; public outcry has forced recalls of automobiles, hair dryers, tampons, canned foods, and appliances, though, tragically, no recalls of DES, thalidomide, kepone, PCBs, Love Canal, or Three Mile Island are possible. Is there a parallel strong concern over new technology which may be harmful to our social and political selves? Precedents on those fronts are far more difficult to find. While the computer cannot be recalled, it can, with tough legislation, remain a servant and not a master. And those who run the machines can be placed in fear of violating the sacred trust of knowing personal information by means of strict laws and strict enforcement.

The privacy issue is nothing new. It is said that the United States government has millions upon millions of files containing personal information on its citizens. Equifax Services, Inc., the country's largest investigations company, is said to have forty million files. Perhaps the advent of the TV-computer merger changes the privacy issue only by degree. But many would argue that the new technology represents a radical departure from past experience. "The social stakes are too high to let the information revolution pass as just another economic opportunity to be resolved by the vagaries of the marketplace."[7]

Most disturbing of all is the prospect that a single entity, corporate or governmental, will control the entire system and its contents. With such control a very real possibility, a book describing American democracy in the new electronic age may already be unnecessary.

Notes

1. Martin Koughan, "The State of the Revolution, 1982," *Channels* 1, no. 5 (December 1981-January 1982): 25.

2. John Wicklein, *Electronic Nightmare* (New York: Viking, 1981), 28.

3. Morris Beja, in Arthur Unger, "Tomorrow's TV in the 1980s: Where You Fit In," *The Christian Science Monitor* 72, no. 240 (November 4, 1980): 13.

4. Wicklein, *Electronic Nightmare*, 197.

5. Anthony Smith, *Goodbye Gutenberg* (New York: Oxford Univ. Press, 1980), 278.

6. Ibid.

7. Harold Sackman, in Wicklein, *Electronic Nightmare*, 6.

9

POLITICAL COMMUNITY

POLITICALLY ACTIVE PEOPLE have always been social, people interacting with each other. Tomorrow's politics is people interacting with machines.

It is extraordinary how the new political realities differ from the old order. Politics was tribe members sitting around a campfire deciding how to divide the newly slain bison. Politics was the debate in the Athenian marketplace over the merits of the Peloponnesian War. Politics was the New England town meeting allocating newly acquired land. Politics was the ward heeler divesting spoils in front of the corner grocery. Politics was a process—a process of settling disputes by arguing, cajoling, discussing, reasoning, trading, and bribing. It was people meeting eyeball to eyeball. Political people were social because they held shared values with others in their neighborhood, city, state, and country. He belonged to institutions—the family, the church, community associations, and civic groups. That is how it has always been, but will it be in the future?

Tomorrow's humanity lives in splendid isolation with its machines. Sure, people living in the video world will have plenty of human contact, especially across the cable. The guy who collects European stamps in Boston will have lots to say to a man with a similar hobby in Boise. The expert on dyslexia in Mobile will be in constant contact with the expert in Minneapolis. The chemist in Portland, Oregon will be chatting electronically with his colleague in Portland, Maine. All these miraculous two-way video exchanges may come at a price.

The danger is loss of community. Historically, our communities are both **geographic and institutional.** There is something intrinsically good about belonging to a neighborhood or civic group. There is something to be gained from coaching the little league or instructing a ballet class. There is something positive about sharing experiences and an environment with others.

The new technology doesn't care a whit about any of that. The time demands are so great and the talents of the machines so seductive that traditional bonds of community may be sacrificed to the new technology. People are to be plugged into the new electronic marvels and not other people. To speculate what this may mean for marriages, children, friendships, neighbors, schools, churches, and all other social institutions which go into the word *community* is outright chilling. It is possible that individuals will have more in common with someone of a like occupation or hobby living on the opposite side of the country than they will with the guy next door. One can envision people being hooked into their specialty, whether it be related to work or recreation, and being oblivious to the geographic and institutional community in their midst. Linkage in society will be vertical—scuba diver and scuba diver; movie buff and movie buff; African violet lover and African violet lover.

"How," said one particularly astute political observer, "does the country hold together? What are the shared values?"[1] When people no longer meet casually at the shopping mall and discuss the horrible potholes, the poor quality of teachers at the local elementary school, or the scoundrels in city hall, something valuable is lost. All human interaction in such a context is by its very nature political. A fleeting exchange about garbage collection may ultimately germinate into a petition drive or a telephone call to a councilman, and may eventually result in government doing something about garbage. And even if it does not, both the community and political process are better off because average people have become involved. No one can really say what great political ideas were born over beer in a pub or during a chance street-corner meeting. The ideas in the U.S. Constitution did not spontaneously appear at the Constitutional convention. Those concepts were simmering in the minds of many for years, even generations. The synthesis at Philadelphia was but the final draft of thoughts which had been batted about at firesides for years.

The new technology can tear away at the fabric of social interaction. The chance meetings on street corners may simply not occur. The two parties may be content to view the latest fall fashions on the home TV set and place an order through the cable catalogue. An idea which might have been born through a happenstance meeting in a shopping mall might never be conceived. If this is allowed to happen, no one in the next generation will miss the street-corner politics. A compromise or consensus that might have smoothed over the rough edges of political conflict might never be achieved, because the two parties might never meet.

The great flaw of the coming video world is that government is in the eye of the beholder. If the beholder wants to see what is tidy and clean, then the mess and filth become invisible. For what is not on the screen does not exist to the citizen of the twenty-first century. Unlike his counterpart in the late twentieth century, before demassified, interactive TV became common, the future viewer will not have to watch conscience-wrenching scenes of famine and squalor. There will always be something pleasant and soothing on the tube.

Compassionate video democracy demands exposure to the unpleasant and unfamiliar. Empathy for the human condition must become part of the political process, if viewers are to avoid retreating into a cocoon of selfishness. Fortunately, the technology offers the opportunity to tune into the lives of the disadvantaged. The viewer and video voter of tomorrow must afford himself the chance to see beyond his set. To squander this opportunity is to lose sight of the ends of a just and humane society. What good is the new technology if it serves only to heighten prejudice and promote self interest?

The paradox is that in a world where the visibility of politicians and ideas has grown and expanded, people are becoming increasingly isolated. "Electronic communication is one means by which the very idea of public life has been put to an end. . . . The mass media infinitely heightens the knowledge people have of what transpires in the society, and they infinitely inhibit the capacity of people to convert that knowledge into political action."[2] The image rises up of man being perpetually bombarded with information and then retreating into a shelter to avoid contact with ideas and people who seem in any way alien. Historically, democracy thrives on people seeking out the opinions of others. Much can be gained from the struggle of ideas. While the technology adds to the sum of available opinions, it also allows people to shut out all undesirable voices and banish unsettling opinions. Sadly, trends which have already taken root in American society such as low political participation, apathy, and alienation could thrive in the soil of the new technology. Video voters must fight the tendency to isolate themselves from the unpleasant and the hostile. The pursuit of intellectual isolation would result in the antithesis of what the technology promises.

The new video technology may be the classic double-edged sword. A society which does not see the dangers as well as the blessings may be injured by that very system. Using the new technology to the advantage of narrow class interest can compromise a free society.

Psychologists say there is a qualitative difference between various forms of communication, observing that there is no substitute for face-to-face communication.[3] When the automobile took the place of foot or carriage travel, people lost some human contact. The intimacy found in meeting with fellow walkers may have been missed by those who lived in the transitional generation—while the automobile was gaining public acceptance. The next generation had no recollection of foot and carriage travel, did not miss the loss of intimacy one bit. This automobile generation accepted, never really questioned, whether or not it was appropriate for people to converse and be with others as they travelled from one place to another.

This speaks to the adaptability of people. Once the video revolution takes place there will be some nostalgia for what the old, existing generation had. That won't last long, just as few mourned the passing of foot travel. Just as people will quickly adapt to reading news across a TV screen, shopping at home and taking college courses through the home computer, so they will adapt to making political decisions from the living room chair. Some people may have misgivings about video town meetings or voting at home, but that will pass with time and increased familiarity. The next generation will welcome the new way of running the political system. It won't know differently.

Just as it is vital to plan today for the technology of tomorrow, it is equally important to preserve for tomorrow those institutions which may easily be left as remnants of today. It has been argued that video democracy is well suited to local government. Large counties, states, and most certainly the national government could not realistically function under a direct democracy. The public should never be allowed to believe that old institutions, which do not use the latest technology, are somehow unworthy. A good political institution is one that adapts to *both* technology and environment. Video democracy and small communities work. In a different environment the combination is politically unsound. Even when video democracy is confined to local government there are enormous dangers. Video democracy does not function in isolation. It is part of a video society, a society where people are electronically linked but, at the same time, increasingly separated in other ways.

The analogy of video democracy and the advent of the automobile can be extended to apply here. Not only did the automobile drastically reduce human communication; it also reduced human contact, just as the video revolution promises to do in politics. When people traveled by foot, they got to know their neighborhood. The automobile placed people in mobile steel cells. There was a deep loss of community. Neighbors became strangers and the neighborhood became a place to drive through, not a place to live in. People drove from home to office or from home to shopping mall. They drove on freeways, in part, to avoid neighborhoods which were not pleasing to look at. All things between home and office and home and shopping mall were to be ignored and feared.[4] There was lessened human growth because people were no longer exposed to anything except what was pleasing. Extensive growth and human advancement can take place in environments different from one's own. The broadened range of travel permitted by the automobile helped create fear of contact with the unknown, such as might be encountered by setting out on foot into another neighborhood.

The dreadful scenario—which must not be allowed to occur—goes like this: Viewers forever watch what is familiar and gives them pleasure, and block out what is unpleasant and unfamiliar. The unknown—people and lifestyles on other channels—becomes something to be feared, like the thought of walking through a supposedly dangerous neighborhood at night. Viewers dare not watch channels with different points of view, like a channel run by Chicanos or homosexuals. They will represent the neighborhood passed by on the freeway, glimpsed from afar, but ignored at all costs. Yes, diversity will exist on the new television; it will be more diverse than anything since the Tower of Babel. If something is only watched by people who are already true believers, then the best interests of democracy are not being served. Like the Tower of Babel there could be a massive breakdown in communication among the dozens of groups on the cable, with each speaking its own language and closing off avenues of communication to all but the most adventurous viewers. Will people watch solely what they want and isolate themselves from the rest of society? That which has traditionally been encompassed by the word *community* may well shrink in size to the family living room. If there is a community beyond the living room, who will seek it out? On the tube there will be no surprises—no stimulus to stir the intellect, imagination or creativity—unless the viewer seeks it out. Otherwise, everyone will be comfortable, secure, and very alone.

If one recalls Locke, it is apparent that any democratic system survives only as long as its citizens continue to reason. The reasoning process can take place across a TV screen, a council chamber extended. This liberal tradition must be allowed to flourish. A society which cloisters itself in a video dreamland abandons reason. A society of reasonable people needs a steady infusion of new ideas and differing points of view. The worst side effects of the next TV era—isolation and loss of community—must be avoided. Tragically, there is an abundance of signs that Locke's voice of reason may be running against the tide of contemporary American culture.

The new video technology is larger than politics. While this discussion has centered on the impact of interactive video on politics and American government, it has not taken an overview.

Clearly, the very character of American society could be changed by the new technology. That analysis is in the realm of psychologists, sociologists, and theologians. The new technology draws a broad brush across the American canvas. Even the most brilliantly contrived and executed video democracy is of minor consequence if the new technology is used to sever the ancient bonds of community.

The core argument of this book is that local government and a direct electronic democracy can serve the highest American ideals. The proposition makes sense, but the entire proposal is worthless if the cultural environment is anticommunity. Whether one is talking about representative government or direct democracy, it is axiomatic that government is only as good, just, and responsive as its citizens.

Turn for a moment to a vision of contemporary America which is anticommunity and therefore a poor risk for video democracy. This is the America of "me" and not "us." For video democracy to work, the cultural environment must value the community over the self.

Reflect on contemporary America, peopled by what author and social critic Tom Wolfe calls the "Me Generation." The world is centered on the self. There is an overconcern, no, an obsession with the health of one's own body and psyche, with a proportionate lack of interest in anything communal. America is thoroughly immersed in a fantasyland of jogging, health foods, aerobics, belly dancing, sex adventures, and any number of psychic therapies. The sales of so-called survival books are booming.[5] The prevailing philosophy is "I'm for me; to hell with you: "

> Having no hope of improving their lives in any of the ways that matter, people have convinced themselves that what matters is psychic self-improvement; getting in touch with their feelings . . . overcoming the "fear of pleasure." Harmless in themselves, these pursuits, elevated to a program and wrapped in the rhetoric of authenticity and awareness, signify a retreat from politics and a repudiation of the recent past.[6]

Americans are ideal recruits for the worst side effects of the video revolution. People who worship at the altar of self-improvement at the expense of family, friends, neighbors, and community will not be good video citizens. They are already depoliticized. Politics calls on the individual to see himself as part of a larger unit. The "Me Generation" asks the individual to look inward. These two orientations are irreconcilable. The video revolution offers the world from the end of a cable—press the magic buttons and all pleasures and self gratification are there.

But the video revolution also offers people the opportunity to revitalize local democracy. It can bring people together to solve community problems. It can personalize politics and government to an extent never imagined. It can restore faith in the system. What the video revolution cannot do is change values. The video world can be only as pristine or corrupt as the world surrounding it. That is why contemporary values should be examined as society embarks on a new association with the television. Look first to the values of society to see where the technology will go.

The video world abhors face-to-face interaction. It asks only to interact with the machine. Just walk down Main Street. Look at the numbers of people with earphones listening to their own music, oblivious to the world about them. The proliferation of the Sony Walkman and similar sound devices is strikingly symbolic. Look at the faces. They are blank. With earphones on, the individual closes out all outside stimuli. He is his own captive audience. Walking down the street the earphoned individual doesn't hear the sounds made by his very own community of sound. He hears nothing but a preselected recording that makes him feel good. There isn't the slightest need to interact with anyone as long as the portable tape recorder is there to block out offending noise and people who would best be seen and silent. This is *precisely* what the new world of television has the potential to do. It can construct an artificial barrier between the individual and his environment; there is no need to experience the real environment as long as there are buttons to push and an unlimited selection of video options. The new video world is self-gratification carried to its technological zenith.

One-time radical Jerry Rubin spoke of his own experience with the American spiritual supermarket: "In five years from 1971 to 1975 I experienced est, gestalt therapy, bioenergetics, rolfing, massage, jogging, health foods, t'ai chi, Esalen, hypnotism, modern dance, meditation, Silva Mind control, Arica, acupuncture, sex therapy, Reichian therapy and More House—a smorgasbord in New Consciousness."[7] All this was in an effort—perhaps futile—to gain insight into the self. Rubin and countless others like him may, in fact, find the level of self-awareness they seek, but they do so at great loss. In effect, Rubin and the others seal themselves off from true social interaction, which has always been the very foundation of society. In all these therapies the theme is essentially the same. The individual is all powerful, all good and totally determines his own fate.[8] Author Peter Marin calls the present age of self-glorification "an embarrassed denial of human reciprocity and community." As people are told there is no such thing as guilt or shame, the notion of community goes down the social drain. Unless people can feel guilt because there is hunger, fear, and injustice in the world, then society is content to wallow in the muck of self-interest. The new therapies "provide adherents with a way to avoid the demands of the world, to smother the tug of conscience."[9]

Live for the moment. It is the clarion call of some Americans giving up on the concept of community. Without a tomorrow and without empathy for one's neighbor, there can be no sense of community. Therapies and philosophies aimed solely at self-actualization and self-realization contribute nothing to the commonweal. There is no building for tomorrow, only the destruction of the present. The moment, of course, lasts but an instant; tomorrow lasts forever. But don't tell that to Werner Erhard, who founded the cult of self-realization called *est*. Collective responsibility is not Erhard's concern; neither is a well-functioning democracy. He wants people to shed the bonds of helping each other within the ancient concept of community. "The self [in est] replaces community, relation, neighbor, chance or god."[10] Erhard might well look upon the burgeoning video world with unabashed awe. How wonderful constantly to gratify yourself and answer to no one. Work, shopping, entertainment—total fulfillment without interacting with anyone, ever.

Jump ahead from today into the new video world. America is already prepared for the short leap into the total video age; Americans are over-eager to embrace the new technology. In fact, it is utterly frightening how much Americans identify with machines. Today's heroes aren't the rugged achievers of old. No, they are human-machines—the Six Million Dollar Man, the Incredible Hulk, the Bionic Woman, C-3PO, R2-D2, and a variety of robots from movies like *Star Wars* and *Battlestar Galactica*.[11]

> This hero robot walks like a man, [is] the perfect slave . . . strong, clean, unable to loaf or talk back [and] promises to liberate mankind from life's dull and dirty jobs. . . . The cult of robot expresses a celebration of powerlessness, a willingness to be led; and it is precisely those gestures which seem most "liberated" that serve this attitude most effectively.[12]

Small wonder among the most popular toys today are the robotlike "Trans-formers" and "Go-bots."

The robot is also the ideal hero for the age of self-gratification. It is devoid of human emotions. The robot wouldn't be the least bit pained by divorce, loss of friendship, or even death. The robot seems totally independent. Is that not what the video revolution promises—a self-contained world where man interacts with machine, where emotion is non-existent and unnecessary, and where man ultimately becomes one with machine? The home computer is virtually another member of the household, so says Madison Avenue.

Americans already speak of themselves as machines. Such common phrases as "wasted" or "burned out" come straight from the electronics factory. So too when one speaks of being able to "function" or of being "together" with "his head straight on."[13] What people are doing is comparing themselves to machines, which is a wonderful comparison for the day when man and machine become interactive partners.

Cults and the myriad of self-help therapies are extensions of the machine-mind. "Self knowledge is a snap when someone else will work it out for you, just as the robot's effectiveness depends entirely on the skills of a repairman."[14] The age of self-glorification can be seen on its mirror side as the age of the man-machine.

Psychologists and social thinkers have given a name to the age of the self—it is called the new narcissism. Narcissus, according to Greek legend, was a beautiful youth who became enamored with his own reflection in a pool and became transfixed until he died. How perfectly the legend of Narcissus fits with a society embarrassed by wrinkles, fearful of old age, and terrified by death. How perfectly the legend fits with encounter sessions where the number one topic is "let's talk about *me*." The ghost of Narcissus roams at will in America. It is found on every avenue of life including the economic and political. Narcissism is found on many a psychiatrist's couch; narcissism in the psychological sense has been identified as a psychic disorder characterized by unhappy people who strive for admiration to counteract inner feelings of humiliation, rage and inferiority.

The cultural side of Narcissism is the facet most related and important to future democracy. Tom Wolfe noted that Americans have not always been followers of the credo of the Me Generation. The nation has not always been inhabited by cultural, if not psychological narcissists. Most people, says Wolfe, "have lived as if they are living their ancestors' lives and their offsprings' lives and perhaps their neighbors' lives as well. They have seen themselves as inseparable from the great tide of chromosomes of which they created and passed on."[15]

The narcissist, who lives by the principle of self as central, cannot accept the concept of mutual dependency, which is the cornerstone of community. The cultural narcissist scrawls on the sides of subway cars with spray paint and escapes reality through the flagrant use of drugs. Some might call him an exhibitionist waving the banner of self. Others might say his unending quest for self-gratification is "an attempt to throw off the chains of civilization."[16] He is crying out for attention, for recognition, for love. The narcissist, however, travels on a one-way street. He has no interest in extending a hand to his neighbor or improving the community. As society has historically cultivated interdependency, the narcissist works at loosening all constraints which bind him to the community as a whole. "It [the pleasure principle] undermines the ability to work at being together at all, let alone work for a living."[17]

In theory, narcissistic societies need not threaten the very survival of the political system. There's hardly a problem when the system is ruled from the top. Monarchy, oligarchy, and dictatorship function regardless of the reigning philosophy of the masses. In fact, the more disinterested the masses are, the easier it is to rule from on high.

What a perfect environment for a dictatorship. Symbolically, everyone has those earphones on. All are blind to the plight of the next guy and, in turn, uncaring about the community as a whole. They could care less about social issues. Not only is the population depoliticized, but it is fragmented. No one is in physical contact with anyone, because each is enslaved by the full-time occupation of self-gratification. In a democracy the individual looks inward and asks if he is accountable for the evils in society. In a dictatorship, the individual is asked not to think about accountability. That's not the citizen's concern. If a society is living the pleasure principle, that society is also lacking a sense of accountability. That's fertile ground for dictatorship.

The pleasure principle as a secular philosophy is far more dangerous in a democracy than in any other form of government. Any system which rests on reciprocity is in serious trouble when the vital links between citizens are severed. The disintegration of national political parties, the inability of parties to retain the loyalty of the masses, low voter turnout, and a strong undercurrent of boredom and alienation with politics bode ill for the ability of the system to ride out the storms of cultural Narcissism.

Mass participation is democracy's counterweight to the forces of authoritarianism. When America becomes a nation of the disinterested and apolitical, it sends out an invitation to those opposed to popular government.

Far from a prudish argument against self-gratification, these words serve to point out that, while the new technology in itself is politically neutral, people are not. The technology itself may well be used by autocrats as by democrats; the hardware contains equal potential for evil as good. The people pushing the buttons and watching the screens, *they* are the ones who will assign moral character to the technology.

The concepts of diversity and community are utterly indispensible to democracy. The new technology can expand one's world or seal it into splendid isolation. Expansion can enhance the prospect for democracy and isolation work to destroy it. The salvation of the democratic system has nothing to do with incorporating video democracy into the political process. Survival depends on citizen vigilance.

Hannah Arendt wrote of the Athenian *polis*, "The principle characteristic of the tyrant was that he deprived the citizen of access to the public realm, where he could show himself and be seen, hear and be heard . . . [the tyrant] confined citizens to the privacy of their households." [18]

Tomorrow's citizen has a choice. He can be part of the public realm or he can retreat into a private video world. In the former, his life becomes filled with the joy of accomplishment and feeling of belonging. In the latter, his life is void of real achievement and sense of community.

For democratic humanity there is no choice.

Notes

1. Peter Marudas, administrative assistant to Sen. Paul S. Sarbanes, Federal Office Building, Baltimore, Maryland, personal interview, May 22, 1981.

2. Richard Sennett, *The Fall of Public Man* (New York: Alfred A. Knopf, 1977), 282-83.

3. Stuart Miller, environmental psychologist, Towson State University, Towson, Maryland, personal interview, July 16, 1981.

4. Ibid.

5. Christopher Lasch, *The Culture of Narcissism* (New York: W. W. Norton & Co., 1978), 4.

6. Ibid.

7. Ibid., 14.

8. Peter Marin, "The New Narcissism," *Harper's* 251, no. 1505 (October 1975): 46.

9. Ibid., 48.

10. Ibid.

11. Mark Miller, "Turned On, Tuned Up, Burned Out," *The Nation* 229, no. 5 (August 25, 1979): 149.

12. Ibid.

13. Ibid., 152.

14. Ibid., 150.

15. Tom Wolfe, *Mauve Gloves & Madmen, Clutter & Vine* (New York: Farrar, Straus and Giroux, 1976), 166.

16. Simon Sobo, "Narcissism and Social Disorder," *The Yale Review* 64, no. 4 (June 1975): 531.

17. Ibid., 534.

18. Hannah Arendt, in Marin, "The New Narcissism," 55.

10

THE NEW DEMOCRACY

AT THE TIME it seemed so simple. Only last week, Mike Smith, the captain of the high school football team, was run down by a crazed driver. The newspaper account said that Smith's death was the result of a motorist high on the hallucinogenic drug PCP. All the neighbors agreed. The video council had to act. At the next video meeting there would be a proposed town law placed before voters. That law would make it illegal for anyone to drive in the community under the influence of drugs. Like many ordinances placed before the video council there was a consensus among voters. The law on drugs and driving would pass.

But it wasn't so simple. True, everyone in town was outraged that a young man was struck by a drugged motorist. The grizzly photograph on the news certainly did much to insure passage of the law. Video democracy always seemed to work best where people empathized with each other's tragedies. Even if citizenship were not a full-time occupation, it certainly consumed a substantial amount of time for many voters.

Soon most people realized that legislating against drugged driving was a rather tricky procedure. How does one define "drugs"? What about the person taking medication? What if someone took too many over-the-counter drugs? What sort of lab or field test could be made for drugs? What would be admissible evidence in court? Can someone be forced to take a blood test? What should be appropriate punishment? What if someone was high on drugs, but not at fault in an accident? What is the legal relationship between drugs and alcohol?

Video democracy does not make the questions before local government **any easier**. It is not the McDonald's of government or the exact change lane of decision making. The complex will always be complex. This town will have to wrestle with the same terribly complex technical and legal questions as an elected town council would have done before the advent of video democracy. Video democracy does nothing to circumvent the agonizing, often wrenching decisions of government. Anyone who believes that plugging a community into a video council somehow changed decision making would be surprised.

Video governments of the future must rely on experts. They must have the same access to the scientist, engineer, lawyer, consultant, physician, or any expert as traditional town councils. But one thing video democracy does is broaden the base of expertise. Everyone can contribute his knowledge and experience. More importantly, video democracy deepens the moral foundation of government. Mass, direct democracy does not have in itself any great insight into the more esoteric questions that come before community governments. With video democracy, there is no barrier against calling upon experts. Direct democracy is not synonymous with government by the ill-informed. If an issue requires study, a committee can be formed to report back to the community at large on the cable at a particular time. Video democracy is not synonymous with snap judgments. It can and should be contemplative. But people can reason without being in the same room; technology has transcended space. Groups can communicate and legislate across a cable as they could across a table.

Clichés about the capacity of direct democracy to deal with the complex forever kept the masses of citizens from the experience of dealing directly with government. Prior to today's technology, there may have been merit to that argument. One can say that in most communities direct democracy is too unwieldy in the absence of a two-way community-based cable system. The old saying that direct democracy is a take it or leave it proposition rings hollow in the context of today's technology.

Video democracy has the same flexibility as conventional local government. It can react to events either rapidly or with great caution; with intelligence or ignorance; with sound judgment or moral speciousness. The quality of government rests on the quality of those who are pushing the buttons.

Direct democracy improves the existing system. The twin pillars of indirect democracy—partisan politics and personal ambition—interfere with reason and common sense. Partisan politics and ambition are necessary evils of the indirect system, but become thoroughly unnecessary in light of the new technology.

With video democracy the decision-making process is unpolluted by the more sordid aspects of indirect democracy. This purging of personal ambition is a powerful incentive to try direct democracy. Since there are no longer any professional politicians, decisions are based more on what is correct for the community than what is right for a politician's future. Video democracy is at once less selfish and more honest in its approach to government. Occasionally, personal ambition and the general good coincide. But why should the commonweal be an afterthought, an add-on to good government? The public has a right to politics uncluttered by personal ambition. Allow all participating citizens to juggle the many competing interests; to decide between two rights; to weigh the technical against the moral; to decide between the fiscally sound and the purely generous. Why leave it to professionals? Why continue to let people build careers at the expense of good government?

The choice is not one of indirect versus direct democracy. There is no single entity called indirect democracy, certainly not on the local level. Some communities have strong mayors, others weak mayors, and many, no mayor at all. Some are intensely partisan and others have no parties. Some have commissioners and others professional managers. Some have councils elected by district; others are elected at large and some have a combination of both. It is impossible to speak of local government as a single widely accepted system. It is many systems— many evolving systems. To dismiss video democracy because it appears unconventional is to deny the enormous diversity of local government throughout the country.

While the national and various state governments are the offspring of constitutions, local governments usually are not. They are often the product of many decades of trial and error; of periods of idealism tempered by years of cynicism. It is only at the local level where Americans have the luxury of continually molding the institution of government. Local government is clay ready to be formed to esthetics of a particular community. What can be more challenging in a free society than to have the power to change the very structure of government? Video democracy is within the most noble tradition of American politics. It provides the ability to play with the form without throwing away the substance of democracy. The overall goal of practical, efficient, honest government is unchanged. Rousseau said man must vote for himself, speak for himself, think for himself, believe for himself—that is the path to freedom.[1] "If a people gives themselves a representative," said Rousseau, "they are no longer free for their laws are no longer self prescribed."[2]

The question arises whether video democracy can be adapted on the state and national levels. The answer is, probably not. There are practical considerations. To tamper with constitutions is to make the state and federal governments political guinea pigs. Obviously, if over a period of time video democracy proves to be a resounding success on the local level, states may want to apply certain aspects of it to their own legislative processes. No doubt, the technology will eventually be used by the states and by Washington to measure public opinion.

Video democracy speaks to the sense of community, of belonging. It should be restricted to a homogeneous area, if possible. Shared values and mutual respect among neighbors make video democracy workable. Lacking these qualities, video democracy can quite literally degenerate into meaningless video chatter. But conventional democracy can become corrupt, authoritarian and otherwise oblivious to public opinion. A solid sense of community can save video democracy from stumbling into the abyss of government by chaos. It is the very mission of a democratic people to experiment continually with ways to expand the base of government.

It is ironic that totalitarian governments adapt more readily to new technology than democracies do. Every major totalitarian regime in this century has used the latest communications technology to control and enhance its power. It can be debated whether a true totalitarian state can exist without controlling all communications. A despot without telephones, radio, TV, and the computer cannot reach into the home, nor can he control the soul. With a hold over these communications technologies, the greatest evil is possible.

Why live in the eighteenth century if a technology exists which can improve on the original product? Technology itself is morally neutral. The morality of any technology turns on the morality of the people using it. The despot will use interactive cable technology far differently from the democrat.

How will the rest of the world respond to American experimentation with direct democracy? It is a most intriguing question. Authoritarian governments will dismiss any extension of democracy as folly. But those regimes value control as a means of achieving stability. To them, freedom becomes anarchy. Video democracy would clearly befuddle the autocrat whether he calls himself comrade or generalissimo.

What of the democratic governments and those other governments throughout the world which aspire to democracy? One must believe that any extension of democracy would serve as a beacon of hope to those who accept as a matter of faith that the people should rule. Even if video democracy is never practiced beyond Main Street, the very existence of direct democracy would be celebrated. In an age when American foreign policy is suspect among democrats, what better way is there to prove this nation's commitment to genuine popular government? The world should see that American democracy is not stagnant, mired in complacency. Video democracy can show the world that the American system can adapt to the new, while retaining its core values.

It is time to move forward. Commissions should be established in every state, perhaps in every county with interactive cable. Begin a dialogue among politicians, educators, technicians, and the general public. Come up with a plan to implement video democracy. Commission plans should address these points:

—Utilizing interactive cable technology for the purpose of running local government.
—Allowing for the free exchange of ideas across the cable.
—Providing for the systematic presentation of issues.
—Setting up a constitutionally legal way of legislating local ordinances using the new video technology.
—Protecting the rights of minorities from the tyranny of the majority.
—Increasing citizen participation in local government.
—Establishing a method for evaluating video democracy.

These guidelines are not only feasible, but also realistic and logical. Communities already served by interactive cable can begin their experimentation with video democracy in short order. There is nothing sacred about mayors, councils, commissioners, or any combination of them. If popular rule is better served by another system, try it.

Our technology affords Americans an opportunity to taste a purer form of democracy; to savor the joy of joining a political community; to revel in the knowledge that democracy can indeed be liberating.

Notes

1. Less Cameron McDonald, *Western Political Theory* (New York: Harcourt, Brace & World, 1962), 217.
2. Ibid. (Rousseau), 210.

BIBLIOGRAPHY

Books

Abraham, Henry J. and Corry, J. A. *Elements of Democratic Government.* New York: Oxford Univ. Press, 1958.

Barber, James David. *Citizen Politics: An Introduction to Political Behavior.* Chicago: Markham Publishing, 1969.

———. *The Pulse of Politics.* New York: Norton Simon, 1980.

———, ed. *Race for the Presidency.* Englewood Cliffs, N.J.: Prentice-Hall, 1978.

Barnouw, Eric. *Tube of Plenty.* New York: Oxford Univ. Press, 1975.

Bathory, Petter Dennis. *Leadership in America.* New York: Longman, Inc., 1978.

Bloom, Melvyn H. *Public Relations and Presidential Campaigns: A Crisis in Democracy.* New York: Thomas Y. Crowell Co., 1973.

Broder, David S. *Changing of the Guard.* New York: Simon and Schuster, 1980.

———. *The Party's Over.* New York: Harper and Row, 1971.

Bryce, James. *The American Commonwealth.* Vols. 1, 2. New York: Macmillan, 1914.

Burlingame, Roger. *The Engines of Democracy.* New York: Scribner & Sons, 1940.

Burnham, Walter Dean. *Critical Elections and the Mainsprings of American Politics.* New York: W. W. Norton & Co., 1970.

Burner, David. "The Democratic Party: 1910-1932." In *History of U.S. Political Parties Vol. III.* Arthur M. Schlesinger, Jr., ed. New York: Chelsea House, 1973.

Burns, James MacGregor. *The Deadlock of Democracy.* Englewood Cliffs, N.J.: Prentice Hall, 1963.

———. *Roosevelt: The Lion and the Fox.* New York: Harcourt, Brace & World, 1956.

Carman, Harry J., Harold C. Syrett, and Bernard W. Wishy. *A History of the American People.* Vols. 1, 2. New York: Alfred A. Knopf, 1960, 1961.

Chambers, William N. and Walter D. Burnham, eds. *The American Party Systems.* New York: Oxford Univ. Press, 1967.

Chute, Marchette. *The First Liberty.* New York: E. P. Dutton & Co., 1969.

Commager, Henry Steele. *The American Mind.* New Haven: Yale Univ. Press, 1950.

Culbert, David Holbrook. *News for Everyman.* Westport, Conn.: Greenwood, 1976.

Dahl, Robert A. *Who Governs?* New Haven: Yale Univ. Press, 1961.

Davis, Harry R. and Robert C. Good, eds. *Reinhold Niebuhr On Politics,* New York: Charles Scribner's Sons, 1960.

Degler, Carl N. *Out of Our Past.* New York: Harper and Row, 1970.

de Grazia, Alfred, *Political Organization,* New York: The Free Press, 1952.

de Tocqueville, Alexis. *Democracy in America.* New York: Vintage Books, 1945. Henry Reeve text, ed. Phillips Bradley.

DeVries, Walter and V. Lance Tarrance. *The Ticket-Splitters.* Grand Rapids, Mich.: William B. Eerdmans, 1972.

Ekrich, Arthur A., Jr. *Progressivism in America.* New York: New Viewpoints, 1974.

Erikson, Robert S. and Norman R. Luttbeg. *American Public Opinion: Its Origins, Content and Impact.* New York: John Wiley & Sons, 1973.

Forbes, Robert James. *Man The Maker.* New York: Abelard-Schuman, 1958.

Forcey, Charles. *The Crossroads of Liberalism.* New York: Oxford Univ. Press, 1961.

Frankel, Charles. *The Democratic Prospect.* New York: Harper and Row, 1962.

Friedrich, Carl J. *The New Belief in the Common Man.* Boston: Little, Brown and Co., 1942.

Fulbright, J. William. "The Elite and the Electorate: Is Government by the People Possible?" In *Challenges to Democracy,* Edward Reed, ed. New York: Frederick A. Praeger, 1963.

Gans, Herbert J. *The Levittowners.* New York: Pantheon Books, 1967.
————. *The Urban Villagers.* New York: The Free Press, 1962.

Goldwin, Robert A., ed. *Political Parties in the Eighties.* Washington, D.C.: American Enterprise Institute for Public Policy Research and Kenyon College, 1980.

Herring, Pendleton. *The Politics of Democracy.* New York: W. W. Norton & Co., 1940.

Hiebert, Ray Eldon, Donald F. Ungurait, and Thomas W. Bohn. *Mass Media.* New York: David McKay, 1974.

Hofstadter, Richard. *The Age of Reform.* New York: Alfred A. Knopf, 1955.
————. *The Idea of a Party System.* Berkeley: Univ. of California Press, 1969.
————, *The Progressive Movement 1900-1915.* Englewood Cliffs, New Jersey, Prentice-Hall, 1963.

Hyneman, Charles C. and Charles E. Gilbert, *Popular Government in America*. New York: Atherton, 1968.

Ippolito, Dennis S. and Thomas G. Walker, *Political Parties, Interest Groups, and Public Policy*. Englewood Cliffs, N.J.: Prentice-Hall, 1980.

Isely, Jeter Allen. *Horace Greeley and The Republican Party, 1853-1861*. Princeton: Princeton Univ. Press, 1947.

Keller, Suzanne. *Beyond the Ruling Class*. New York: Random House, 1963.

Key, V. O., Jr. *Public Opinion and American Democracy*. New York: Alfred A. Knopf, 1964.

Koenig, Louis W. *Bryan*. New York: G. P. Putnam's Sons, 1971.

Kristol, Irving and Paul H. Weaver, eds. *The Americans: 1976*. Lexington, Mass.: Lexington Books, 1976.

Ladd, Everett Carll, Jr. *Where Have All the Voters Gone?* New York: W. W. Norton & Co., 1977.

—— and Charles D. Hadley. *Transformations of the American Party System*. New York, W. W. Norton & Co., 1975.

Lane, Robert E. *Political Ideology*. New York: The Free Press, 1962.

Lasch, Christopher. *The Culture of Narcissism*. New York: W. W. Norton & Co., 1978.

Lee, Alfred McClung. *The Daily Newspaper in America*. New York: Octagon Books, 1973.

Lerner, Max. *America As A Civilization*. New York: Simon and Schuster, 1957.

Leuchtenburg, William. "The Roosevelt Reconstruction: Retrospect." In *Understanding the American Experience Vol. II*, James M. Banner, Jr., Sheldon Hackney, and Barton J. Bernstein, eds. New York: Harcourt Brace Jovanovich, 1973.

Levine, Andrew. *Liberal Democracy: A Critique of Its Theory*. New York: Columbia Univ. Press, 1981.

Lipset, Seymour Martin. *The First New Nation*. New York: Basic Books, 1963.

Lipson, Leslie. *The Democratic Civilization*. New York: Oxford Univ. Press, 1964.

Livingston, John C. and Robert G. Thompson. *The Consent of the Governed*. New York: Macmillan, 1971.

McCraw, Thomas K. "The Progressive Legacy." In *The Progressive Era*, Lewis L. Gould, ed. Syracuse, N.Y.: Syracuse Univ. Press, 1974.

McDonald, Lee Cameron, *Western Political Theory*, New York: Harcourt, Brace & World, 1962.

McGinniss, Joe. *The Selling of the President 1968*. New York: Pocket Books (Simon and Schuster), 1969.

MacIver, R. M. *The Web of Government*. New York: The Free Press, 1965.

McLuhan, Marshall. *Understanding Media*. New York: Signet Books, 1964.

Mann, Arthur, ed. *The Progressive Era*. New York: Holt, Rinehart and Winston, 1963.

Manuel, Frank E., ed. *Utopias and Utopian Thought*. Boston: Houghton Mifflin, 1966.

Mayer, Andre and Michael Wheeler. "Referendum Fever." In *New Alignments in American Politics*. Carl Lowe, ed. New York: H. W. Wilson Co., 1980.

Mayer, George H. "The Republican Party 1932-1952." In *History of U.S. Political Parties Vol. III*. Arthur M. Schlesinger, Jr., ed. New York: Chelsea House, 1973.

Michels, Robert. *Political Parties*. New York: Dover Publications, 1959 (original English translation, 1915).

Milbrath, Lester W. *Political Participation*. Chicago: Rand McNally, 1965.

Mills, C. Wright. *Power, Politics and People*. New York: Oxford Univ. Press, 1963.

Minar, David W. *Ideas and Politics: The American Experience*. Homewood, Ill.: The Dorsey Press, 1964.

Mott, Frank Luther. *American Journalism: A History: 1690-1960*. New York, Macmillan, 1962.

Mumford, Lewis. *The City in History*. New York: Harcourt, Brace & World, 1961.

Nevins, Allan. *The Evening Post*. New York: Boni and Liveright, 1922.

Nimmo, Dan D. and James E. Combs, *Subliminal Politics*. Englewood Cliffs, N.J.: Prentice-Hall, 1980.

O'Brien, Frank M. *The Story of The Sun*. New York: D. Appleton and Co., 1928.

Ogle, Marbury B., Jr. *Public Opinion and Political Dynamics*. Cambridge, Mass.: The Riverside Press, 1950.

Polsby, Nelson W. and Aaron B. Wildavsky, *Presidential Elections*. New York: Charles Scribner's Sons, 1971.

Pomper, Gerald M. "The Decline of the Party in American Elections." In *New Alignments in American Politics*. Carl Lowe, ed. New York: H. W. Wilson Co., 1980.

Pye, Lucian W., ed. *Communications and Political Development*. Princeton, Princeton Univ. Press, 1963.

Ranney, Austin and Willmore Kendall. *Democracy and the American Party System*. New York: Harcourt, Brace and Co., 1956.

Reed, Edward. *Challenges to Democracy*. (For the Center for the Study of Democratic Institutions). New York: Frederick A. Praeger, 1964.

Roll, Charles W. and Albert H. Cantril, *Polls: Their Use and Misuse in Politics*. Cabin John, Md.: Seven Locks Press, 1980.

Rose, Arnold W. *The Power Structure*. New York: Oxford Univ. Press, 1967.

Schattschneider, E. E. *Party Government*. Westport, Conn.: Greenwood, 1942.

Sennett, Richard. *The Fall of Public Man*. New York: Alfred A. Knopf, 1977.

Sigel, Efrem, ed. *Videotext*. New York: Harmony Books, 1980.

Silbey, Joel H. *The Transformation of American Politics, 1840-1860*. Englewood Cliffs, N.J.: Prentice-Hall, 1967.

Small, William. *To Kill a Messenger*. New York: Hastings House, 1974.

Smith, Anthony. *Goodbye Gutenberg*. New York: Oxford Univ. Press, 1980.

Sorauf, Frank J. *Party Politics in America*. Boston: Little, Brown and Co., 1968.

———. *Political Parties in the American System*. Boston: Little, Brown and Co., 1964.

Spero, Robert. *The Duping of the American Voter*. New York: Lippincott & Crowell, 1980.

Sundquist, James L. "The Realignment of the 1930s." In *Presidential Politics*. James I. Lengle and Byron E. Shafer, eds. New York: St. Martin's, 1980.

Toffler, Alvin, Future Shock. New York: Bantam Books, 1970 Originally published by Random House, 1971.

———. *The Third Wave*. New York: William Morrow & Co., 1980.

Weissberg, Robert. *Public Opinion and Popular Government*. Englewood Cliffs, N.J.: Prentice-Hall, 1976.

White, Theodore H. *The Making of the President 1960*. New York: Atheneum, 1961.

———. *The Making of the President 1968*. New York: Atheneum, 1969.

Wicklein, John, *Electronic Nightmare*. New York: Viking, 1981.

Willis, John T. *Presidential Elections in Maryland*, Mt. Airy, MD: Lomond Publications, Inc., 1984.

Wilson, James Q. "American Politics Then and Now." In *New Alignments in American Politics*. Carl Lowe, ed. New York: H. W. Wilson Co., 1980.

Wolfe, Tom. *Mauve Gloves & Madmen, Clutter & Vine*. New York: Farrar, Straus and Giroux, 1976.

Journals

"Abraham Lincoln: Unfinished Business." Editorial *America* 110, no. 6, (February 8, 1964).

Anderson, Kevin, "Electronic Mail Firms in Survival Fight," *U.S.A. Today*, March 11, 1985.

"And Now, Live From Capitol Hill, Your Congress at Work." *Nation's Business* 67, no. 5 (May 1979).

"Another Side to QUBE." *Broadcasting* 100, no. 2 (January 12, 1981).

"Apocalypse Now & Again." *Newsweek* 95 (March 31, 1980).

Armstrong, Richard. "Gutter Politics in the Global Village." *National Review* 36, no. 7 (April 20, 1984).

Baker, Keith Michael. "To Be Free and Still Belong." Book review: *Rousseau: Dreamer of Democracy*, by James Miller. *New York Times*, September 16, 1984.

Barnouw, Erik. "So You Think TV Is Hot Stuff." *Smithsonian* 7, no. 4 (July 1976).

Baruch, Ralph M. "Five Minutes to Countdown." *Vital Speeches* 46, no. 18 (July 1, 1980).

———. "Lifestyle Revolutions in the Television Age." *Vital Speeches* 46, no. 7 (January 15, 1980).

Bernstein, Peter W. "The Race to Feed Cable TV's Maw." *Fortune* 103, no. 9 (May 4, 1981).

———. "Television's Expanding World." *Fortune* 99, no. 13, (July 2, 1979).

Bers, Trudy Haffron. "Local Political Elites: Men and Women on Boards of Education." *The Western Political Quarterly* 31, no. 3 (September 1978).

Bode, Ken. "The Perils of Polling." *The New Republic* 174, no. 3 (January 17, 1976).

Bowie, John. "Power to the People." *National Review* 30, no. 23 (June 9, 1978).

Brown, Les. "The Reinvention of the Television." *AFTRA* 14, no. 3 (Spring 1981).

Brown, Merrill. "A Boom Industry Free to Call Its Shots." *The Washington Post*, January 12, 1981.

"Cable," *Broadcasting Yearbook 1985*, Taishoff, Lawrence B., publisher, Washington, D.C. 1985.

"Cable Connects With Viewers." *USA Today*, December 3, 1984.

"Cable Television in the Eighties." *Emmy* 2, no. 4 (Fall 1980).

"Cable TV's Promise: You're Going to See More of Everything." *U.S. News and World Report* 96 (February 13, 1984).

"Cable TV: The Race to Plug In." *Business Week*, December 8, 1980.

Carmines, Edward and James Stimson. "The Two Faces of Issue Voting." *American Political Science Review* 74, no. 1 (March 1980).

Carmody, Deirdre. "First U.S. Experiments in Electronic Newspapers Begin in Two Communities." *The New York Times*, July 7, 1980.

"CBS, AT & T Begin Text Market Test." *Broadcasting* 103, no. 14 (October 4, 1982).

Ciardi, John. "Black Man in America." *Saturday Review* 46, no. 27 (July 16, 1963).

Clymer, Adam. "Studies Find Future in Political Parties." *The New York Times*, April 20, 1981.

Coates, Joseph F. "Why The People Are Scared." *Vital Speeches* 46, no. 6 (January 1, 1980).

"Competition of New Media." *Broadcasting* 100, no. 2 (January 12, 1981).

Crespi, Irving. "Manipulating Public Opinion." *Society* 13, no. 6 (September/October 1976).

Crossman, Rt. Hon. RHS, MP. "The Politics of Viewing." *New Statesman* 76, no. 1962 (October 18, 1968).

Crouse, Timothy. "How Many Polls Does It Take To Make A President?" *Esquire* 85, no. 4 (April 1976).

"CTAM's Grand Slam." *Broadcasting* 100, no. 10 (March 9, 1981).

"Do Polls Help Democracy?" *Time* 91, no. 22 (May 31, 1968).

Eirinberg, Alan. "It's New: Banking at Home." *Advertising Age*, August 11, 1980.

"Electoral Values Old and New." *Saturday Review* 54, no. 22 (May 29, 1971).

Eller, J. N. "A New Time for Lawmaking." *America* 108, no. 24 (June 15, 1963).

"Emancipation II." Editorial. *America* 108, no. 22 (June 1, 1963).

Emery, Edwin. "Changing Role of the Mass Media in American Politics." *The Annals of the American Academy of Political and Social Science* 427 (September 1976).

Fairlie, Henry. "Sweet Nothings." *The New Republic* 176, no. 4 (June 11, 1977).

Fielding, Cecelia, and William C. Porter, "Time to Turn on the Newspaper." *The Quill* 69, no. 4 (April 1981).

Finifter, Ada W. and Paul R. Abramson, "City Size and Feelings of Political Competence." *Public Opinion Quarterly* 39, no. 2 (Summer 1975).

Frank, Ronald E. and Marshall G. Greenberg, "Zooming in on TV Audiences." *Psychology Today* 13, no. 5 (October 1979).

Gallup, George. "Pollsters, Not Prophets." *Society* 13, no. 6 (September/October 1976).

Gelman, Eric. "The Video Revolution." *Newsweek* 104, no. 6 (August 6, 1984).

Gitlin, Todd. "Rate the Debate." *The Nation* 231 (November 8, 1980).

Glickman, Harvey. "Viewing Public Opinion in Politics: A Common Sense Approach." *Public Opinion Quarterly* 23, no. 4 (Winter 1959).

Gottfried, John. "A Man's Best Friend is His Home Computer." *Saturday Review* 6, no. 20 (October 13, 1979).

Gray, Harry J. "The Electronics Revolution and You." *Vital Speeches* 46, no. 20 (August 1, 1980).

Harwood, Edwin. "The Pluralist Press." *Society* 15, no. 1 (November/December 1977).

Holsendolph, Ernest. "Tougher Times for Cable TV." *The New York Times*, July 11, 1982.

"The Home Information Revolution." *Business Week*, June 29, 1981.

"Home Telecommunications Paths of Growth in the 1980s." *The Futurist* 13, no. 3 (June 1979).

Hurley, Neil P. "The Wired Home, An Information Utility." *America* 139, no. 18 (December 2, 1978).

Hurly, Paul. "The Promises and Perils of Videotex." *The Futurist* 19, no. 2 (April 1985).

"If You're Making a Date With the New Media, Try On the Mid '80s For Size." *Variety*, September 24, 1980.

"Is Cable TV Losing Its Luster?" *U.S. News & World Report* no. 22 (November 22, 1982).

Johnson, Lyndon B. "The Right to Vote." *Vital Speeches* 31, no. 12 (April 1, 1965).

Jones, Robert A. "Public Access TV: Channel 12 Doing the Unexpected." *The Los Angeles Times*, February 22, 1981.

Just, Marion R. "Political Polling and Political Television." *Current History* 67, no. 396 (August 1974).

Kaplan, Peter W. "The Inevitable Machine." *Esquire* 110 (October 1983).

King, Martin Luther, Jr. "Civil Rights No. 1—The Right to Vote." *New York Times Magazine*, March 14, 1965.

————. "Why We Can't Wait." *Saturday Review* 47, no. 22 (May 30, 1964).

Kitman, Marvin. "Dial 900 for President." *The New Leader* 67, no. 3 (February 6, 1984).

Kondracke, Morton. "The Big Swing." *The New Republic*, October 22, 1984.

Koughan, Martin. "The State of the Revolution, 1982." *Channels* 1, no. 5 (December 1981-January 1982).

Levy, Steven. "Speak Up Columbus." *Panorama* 2, no. 2 (February 1981).

Lipset, Seymour Martin. "Is Carter Sure to Win?" *Society* 13, no. 6 (September/October 1976).

"Lowering the Voting Age—Why Not?" Editorial. *America* 122, no. 10 (May 14, 1970).

Madron, Thomas. "Political Parties in the 1980s." *The Futurist* 13, no. 6 (December 1979).

McWilliams, Carey. "Second Thoughts." *The Nation* 229, no. 20 (December 15, 1979).

Marbach, William. "The Dish vs. the Cable." *Newsweek* 101, no. 23 (June 6, 1983).

———— and William J. Cook, "The Revolution in Digitech," 105, no. 11 (March 18, 1985).

Marin, Peter. "The New Narcissism." *Harper's* 251, no. 1505 (October 1975).

Mathias, Charles McC., Jr. "Frank Talk on the Two Party System." *The Nation* 221, no. 22 (December 27, 1975).

Meadows, Edward. "Why TV Sets Do More in Columbus, Ohio." *Fortune* 102, no. 7 (October 6, 1980).

Meredith, Dennis. "Future World of Television—Another 'Revolution' Coming." *Science Digest* 88, no. 3 (September 1980).

Miller, Mark Crispin. "Turned On, Turned Up, Burned Out." *The Nation* 229, no. 5 (August 25, 1979).

Miller, Vernon F. "The Town Meeting Reborn." *Saturday Review* 49, no. 30 (July 23, 1966).

Morrow, Lance. "The Decline of Parties." *Time* 112, no. 21 (November 20, 1978).

Nelson, Michael. "Power to the People." *Saturday Review* 6, no. 23 (November 24, 1979).

"Network Dominance Picked to Continue." *Broadcasting* 100, no. 16 (April 20, 1981).

"The New Constituency." *The Nation* 211, no. 1 (July 6, 1970).

New York Times, October 16, 1920.

————, October 17, 1920.

Nisbet, Robert. "Public Opinion Versus Popular Opinion." *The Public Interest* no. 41 (Fall 1975).

"Now What?" *The New Republic*, November 26, 1984.

Pace, Eric. "Videotex: Luring Advertisers." *New York Times*, October 14, 1982.

Panero, Hugh. "Wily Video Clubs Find Ways to Thrive." *Watch* 1, no. 7 (July 1980).

Patterson, Thomas E. and Robert D. McClure, "Television and the Less Interested Voter." *The Annals of the Academy of Political Science* 425 (May 1976).

Phillips, Kevin. "Controlling Media Output." *Society* 15, no. 1 (November/December 1977).

Pollack, Andrew, "Enhancing Phone Lines," *The New York Times*, March 21, 1985.

"Push Button Democracy Unlikely." *Intellect* 106, no. 2392 (January 1978).

Rabinowitz, George, Paul-Henri Gurian, and Stuart MacDonald. "The Structure of Presidential Elections and the Process of Realignment." *American Journal of Political Science* 28, no. 4 (November 1984).

Roper, Burns W. "Misleading Measurements." *Society* 13, no. 6 (September/October 1976).

"The Rush Into Cable TV Is Now Turning Into a Retreat." *Business Week*, October 17, 1983.

Saldich, Anne R. "Elections in Democracy." *Vital Speeches* 46, no. 16 (June 1, 1980).

Sale, Kirkpatrick. "Why Voters Don't Care." *The Nation* 230, no. 21 (May 31, 1980).

Satow, Roberta. "Pop Narcissism." *Psychology Today* 13, no. 5 (October 1979).

Scanlon, Robert G. "The Year 2,000." *Vital Speeches* 46, no. 23 (September 15, 1980).

Schaefer, Mary Tonne, "Canada's Telidon Technology: In Videotex Vanguard," *Information Retrieval & Library Automation* 20, no. 1 (June 1984).

——, "France's Market Survey of Videotex Use: May to July 1984," *Information Retrieval & Library Automation* 20, no. 9 (February 1985).

——, "Quo Vadis Videotex?" *Information Retrieval & Library Automation* 19, no. 12 (May 1984).

——, "Videotex in the United States," *Information Retrieval & Library Automation* 20, no. 2 (July 1984).

Schlesinger, Arthur, Jr. "The Crisis of the Two-Party System." *Current* 214 (July/August 1979).

Schrage, Michael. "Goodbye 'Dallas,' Hello Videodiscs." *New York* 13, no. 45 (November 17, 1980).

Shales, Tom. "Television in the '80s." *Current* no. 205 (September 1978).

Shapiro, Robert and Benjamin Page. "Effects of Public Opinion On Policy." *The American Political Science Review* 77, no. 1 (March 1983).

Shorris, Earl. "Market Democracy." *Harper's* 257, no. 1542 (November 1978).

Sloan, Allan and Thomas Baker, "AT&T Versus Cable: War of the Wires." *Forbes* 127, no. 10 (May 11, 1981).

Smith, Desmond. "Mining the Golden Spectrum." *The Nation* 228, no. 20 (May 26, 1979).

Smith, Lee. "The Boom in Polls." *Dun's Review* 103, no. 4 (April 1974).

Smith, Ralph Lee. "Plugging Into the New Technology." *The Nation* 233, no. 10 (October 3, 1981).

Smith, Paula. "Cable TV Comes of Age." *Dun's Review* 107, no. 6 (June 1976).

Smith, Stephen A. "Communication and Technology: The Future of American Democracy." *Vital Speeches* 51, no. 2 (November 1, 1984).

Snyder, Richard A. "Democracy: Ills and Cures." *Vital Speeches* 48, no. 21 (August 15, 1982).

"Spring Brings New Technology Exhibition to Capitol Hill." *Broadcasting* 100, no. 13 (March 30, 1981).

Sobo, Simon. "Narcissism and Social Disorder." *The Yale Review* 64, no. 4 (June 1975).

Stone, Clarence. "Local Referendums: An Alternative to the Alienated Voter Model." *Public Opinion Quarterly* 29, no. 2 (Summer 1965).

Talese, Gay. "Selma: Bitter City in the Eye of a Storm." *The New York Times*, March 14, 1965.

"Ted Bates Study Sees Cable Cut of Web Shares." *Variety*, September 24, 1980.

Tesh, Sylvia. "In Support of 'Single Issue' Politics." *Political Science Quarterly* 99, no. 1 (Spring 1984).

"Thar's Gold In Those Cities." *Broadcasting*, March 31, 1980.

Thomas Whiteside, "Onward and Upward with the Arts—Cable III," *The New Yorker*, vol. 61, (June 3, 1985).

Tobin, Richard L. "What Will the 135 Million Do?" *Saturday Review* 54, no. 41 (October 9, 1971).

Toffler, Alvin. "Toward a New Kind of Man." *Current* 222 (May 1980).

Tuchman, Gaye. "Mass Media Values." *Society* 14, no. 1 (November/December 1976).

"TV to Homevideo, 1980-1985." *Variety* September 24, 1980.

Unger, Arthur. "TV: A Trip to the Heartland of Future TV Today." *The Christian Science Monitor* 72, no. 240 (November 5, 1980).

"The Use of CONSENSOR in Televised Town Meetings." Consensor Briefs, Applied Futures, Inc., Greenwich, Connecticut, 06830. Courtesy of W. W. Simmons, president, February 1, 1980.

Vail, Hollis. "Taking Charge of Television." *The Futurist* 13, no. 5 (October 1979).

"Videotex." *The New Yorker* 59 (July 8, 1983).

Vorspan, Albert. "The First Liberty: A History of the Right to Vote." Book Review. *America* 52, no. 21 (May 24, 1969).

Wachtel, Paul L. "The Politics of Narcissism." *The Nation* 232, no. 1 (January 3, 1981).

Waters, Harry. "Cable TV: Coming of Age." *Newsweek* 98, no. 8 (August 24, 1981).

"What Is All This About Cable." *The Dial.* (Public Broadcasting Communications, New York) 2, no. 7 (July 1981).

"What's Ahead for Cable." *Broadcasting* 100, no. 1 (January 5, 1981).

Wheeler, Michael. "Primaries and Opinion Polls." *The Atlantic* 229, no. 5 (May 1972).

Wicklein, John. "Wired City, USA." *The Atlantic* 243, no. 2 (February 1979).

"Will Knight-Ridder Make News With Videotex?" *Business Week*, August 8, 1983.

Witcover, Jules. "Can We Believe the Pollsters?" *The Reporter* 38, no. 10 (May 16, 1968).

Woodward, Kenneth L. and Rachel Mark. "The New Narcissism." *Newsweek* 91, no. 5 (January 30, 1978).

"Young at Heart." *Newsweek* 75, no. 26 (June 29, 1970).

INDEX